"At once witty and vulnerable, Jess ⟨...⟩ :h of air. In *I Could Use a Nap and a Million Dollars*, ⟨...⟩ .de the curtain, welcoming us to look at the reality of her life. She puts an arm around our shoulders and says, 'You aren't alone.'"

Susie Finkbeiner, best-selling author of the Pearl Spence novels

"Jessie uses humor, charm, and the perfect blend of truth and grace to help us deal with the stress that's been snitching our joy. She inflates the small tortures of daily life just enough to get us laughing. Then she infuses powerful truths from God's Word to get us thinking. If you could use a nap or a million dollars, you'll find just what you need in these pages."

Shannon Popkin, author of *Control Girl*

"Jessie has the incredible gift of talking about the most important issues in our lives (which can also be the most frustrating and tear-inducing) in a way that will make you chuckle, maybe even snort, and say, 'Yes, sister. I can survive this, with Jesus's help. Hallelujah. Amen.' She will take you to the deepest places in your heart, but in a manner so disarming you'll stop mid-paragraph and think, 'How did we get here?' But you'll be so glad she took you there, and you'll be better and less stressed because of it."

Amelia Rhodes, author of *Pray A to Z: A Practical Guide to Pray for Your Community*

I Could Use a Nap and a Million Dollars

Biblical Alternatives to Stressed-Out Living

JESSIE CLEMENCE

Kregel
Publications

I Could Use a Nap and a Million Dollars: Biblical Alternatives to Stressed-Out Living
© 2018 by Jessie Clemence

Published by Kregel Publications, a division of Kregel Inc., 2450 Oak Industrial Dr. NE, Grand Rapids, MI 49505.

Published in association with the literary agency of Credo Communications, LLC, Grand Rapids, Michigan, www.credocommunications.net.

To protect the privacy of individuals, some names and identifying details have been changed.

ISBN 978-0-8254-4487-6

Printed in the United States of America
18 19 20 21 22 23 24 25 26 27 / 5 4 3 2 1

For Monday night small group:
I can't begin to explain how much joy you've brought to our lives.
Thanks for teaching us that "authentic community" isn't just a phrase hipsters use to sound fancy. We love you, we love your children, and we can't wait to see what God has in store for you next.

Contents

Dear Stressed-Out Woman with a Twitch in Her Eye

HEY, YOU THERE.

Pardon me for a moment, but I see you.

I see you in my small group, at Target, and across the street. I see you carrying a diaper bag and trying to grab little hands before they dart away, or maybe carrying a briefcase while your cell phone is smashed up against your ear. And I see you carefully choosing your words as you face off in another "heated conversation" with your husband, hoping you don't accidentally say all the things building up inside.

I know your bank account is empty for the third time this month and the car is making a funny squealing sound every time you turn left. I can hear that kid in your back seat screaming *from here*, and I know you're about to lose your mind.

You're worried you're a bad mom and a horrible wife and a lousy Christian too. Sanctified women don't hide in the bathroom from their families, do they?

Why yes, ma'am. They do. They most surely do.

So even if you're hiding in that bathroom right this little minute, I see you. And I'm glad you're here. Together we can sort this all out. We're going to get through this, I pinkie promise.

Just hang on for a few more pages, and we'll find a way through this mess . . .

Jess

Chopping Lettuce and Screeching a Little

Where It All Began

THE MELTDOWN OCCURRED, as many meltdowns do, in the kitchen. One minute I was chopping lettuce, and the next minute I was screeching.

"*How much?* He charged us *how much?*"

"Ninety dollars," Eric said calmly. He was peering out the window to see if the water heater repairman could hear my screeching. Of course the guy could hear me—the neighbors two houses down could probably hear me. I didn't care. I *wanted* him to know how upset I was. (From a distance—I may have some issues with confrontation.) "I just wrote him a check and didn't argue," Eric finished.

I believe this is the point where I burst into hot, slobbery tears in front of my kitchen sink. The children watched with wide eyes, obviously intrigued but also worried. Mom was having a breakdown in the middle of chopping the vegetables. It was a terrible, novel experience for them both.

The repairman had been in our house for less than two hours to find out why our water heater, which was only two years old, was making popping noises. Through the magic of Google, we'd determined it probably had something to do with mineral buildup from hard water. We would have fixed the issue ourselves, but we were already armpit-deep in maintenance issues with our rental house. Our tenant had recently moved out and we'd decided to put it on the market. The exit proceedings, the cleanup, and the expensive repairs had pushed us past our wits' end.

Also, a cold snap breezed into our Michigan February and the temperatures plummeted to seventeen below zero, which coincided with the exact time the rental house's furnace stopped igniting. Eric discovered this minutes before a real estate agent arrived for a showing. The house was about twenty degrees, the air was filled with the smell of gas overflowing from the non-working furnace, and the pipes had all frozen. Even the toilet. *The toilet was frozen.* The furnace repair cost hundreds of dollars, and of course that showing was a bust. Who was going to buy a house that was literally freezing and smelled like gas?

Honestly, it would have been a mercy if an errant spark had ignited all that gas and the house had exploded off the foundation.

But explode it did not, which meant we still owned two houses. When the water heater at our regular house started acting up, we were well past our capacity for dealing with stupid maintenance issues. Henceforth, we called the repairman.

He arrived in our basement and, for some reason I still don't understand, opened the water valve to refill the heater. It had taken us hours to drain the thing, which I'd explained to him when he walked in the door. He filled it back up and then started draining it. While he sat on a five-gallon bucket and waited for it to empty, he conferred over the phone with his boss.

I was obviously twitchy and out of sorts, because he looked at me like I might be mentally unstable and said, "You probably heard that conversation. My boss says you need a whole new heater. There's nothing we can do."

I blinked and summoned my most calm voice. "But it's only two years old. It heats water just fine. It's just making that *noise.*"

"Yeah, well, we can't do anything about that mineral buildup. It'll be cheaper for you to just buy a whole new heater."

Luckily, my husband arrived home and I met him at the door. I hissed a summary of the situation and then went upstairs to deal with dinner, leaving Eric to handle the insanity in the utility room. I will never be as calm and steady as Eric, no matter what kind of prescription medications I'm ingesting, so this was the best situation for everyone in the house. Eric and the guy already knew each other from the aforementioned furnace problem, so they chatted while the man did, well, nothing. Nothing except drain the water *he put into the tank*. Eric refused the new heater, told the man we'd take it from there, and wrote him a check.

And now we're back where we started this story, with me shouting and blubbering in the kitchen.

Adulthood is just so hard. So mind-numbing and hard. How much pressure can one woman take before she starts screaming about the water heater? For the record, that evening we bought six gallons of white vinegar, poured it into the water heater, and then fired it back up. It works just fine. No more popping. The basement smelled like pickles for a few days, but that seemed like a fair price to pay.

The rental house sold soon after (thank you, Lord) and things quieted back down. We rebuilt our savings account and threaded our shredded nerves back together. But we know the next crazy mess is probably just around the corner, crouched and ready to spring. It'll hit us when we least expect it.

Maybe you've never had a screaming fit about a water heater while you chop lettuce. Even so, I bet you can relate. I'm certain you have your own stories of broken-down appliances, job problems, relationship stress, overburdened schedules, and some cranky person who keeps looking at you with disdain, wondering when you're going to get your life together.

Maybe it's Aunt Edna, who married well and doesn't understand why you can't afford private school for your children. Maybe it's your college roommate, who is getting her doctorate and thinks you should get a real job and stop baking cookies with your children all day. It could even be your sister, who does stay home to blissfully bake cookies all day and thinks you should quit your job to focus on more important things. Well, things *she* thinks are more important.

Why does everyone have all these expectations of us? Why can't they just leave us alone? If we have a job, we feel pressure to work harder and climb the career ladder. If we have a career and a family, the head of the PTA makes us feel like we're sacrificing our family for the sake of our job. At the same time, we feel like our boss is unhappy when we need to make family time a priority. We can't win.

We'll never feel thin enough, pretty enough, or fashionable enough. Our cars will never be new enough and our bathtubs will always have that ring. We lie awake at night, worried we'll die in our sleep and our mother will arrive at our house and see that scummy ring in the tub.

This is why we eat too much chocolate and cry in the shower. This is why we need a nap and a million dollars to fall out of the sky. We've had enough. Life is just too much.

> This is why we eat too much chocolate and cry in the shower. . . . Life is just too much.

But—this is exciting, my friend—what if there is another way? Are we here on earth to fall victim to our stress? What if life doesn't have to be about pinched, strained existences? What if we can refocus our attention from our stress to the abundant life Jesus came to bring us? I think it's possible, and I think it's necessary. We need to stop worrying so much about Aunt Edna's expectations and look for God's expectations instead.

Does God command us to have our kids in an expensive private school? No. Did Jesus tell his disciples to work their way up the career ladder? No. Does the Holy Spirit whisper that we must keep our family and our boss perfectly happy at every moment, risking our mental health in the process?

No, ma'am. The Bible does not teach us any of these things. But the Bible does teach us a lot about God's grace-filled expectations and standards. It speaks a lot about having our hearts in the right place so our actions follow. It talks about rest and peace and finding God's provision in the middle of messy, unexpected, and chaotic life.

I wish I could have remembered all this in the middle of my kitchen that day. I wish I'd thought of the beautiful sign my friend Jen painted for my office. It has a silhouette of a little bird on a branch, with the phrase "act justly, love mercy, walk humbly" lettered in the corner. Taken from Micah 6:8, these are the standards God sets for his people. "O people, the LORD has told you what is good, and this is what he requires of you: to do what is right, to love mercy, and to walk humbly with your God."

What a sweet, blessed relief. What grace, written right there in the middle of Micah and hanging on my office wall. I can do those things! I can choose justice and mercy and walk humbly with my Father. But I also need this written on the walls of my heart, so the next time the water heater starts popping and Aunt Edna posts another article to Facebook about the deplorable state of public education, I can be ready with the right perspective. My heart needs to know God's expectations, but it also needs to know that he is able and willing to help me meet every challenge. The pressure is off me. It's off you too. We don't have to handle this all on our own.

Further along in the book, Micah 7:7 says, "As for me, I look to the LORD for help. I wait confidently for God to save me, and my God will certainly hear me." I want Micah's approach. I want to be confident that God will help, that he hears, and that he saves. The entire Bible is full of examples when God stepped in to take the burdens off his people. He sent manna in the wilderness. He sent Jesus as the sacrifice for our sins so we could live in communion with him. He sent the Holy Spirit to comfort and teach us day by day.

And I also believe it's possible he sent ice cream so we could hide in our closets with a hot fudge sundae when the days get really, really rough. Not that I know this from personal experience, of course. (I usually drive someplace to get my ice cream and then eat it right in the van before anyone sees. Thank you for not judging me.)

So the expectations and the pressures can do their worst. They can hound and attack us and make us feel like we're pitiful wrecks who can't do anything right. But that doesn't mean we have to pay them any attention. God's Word tells another story, one we'd be wise to seek.

We're going to be looking for his story and perspective in response to all the different kinds of stress life throws at us. When I was first gathering ideas for this book, I turned to my friends. Thanks to the magic of the internet, I can interview more than five hundred people simultaneously, so I threw out this question on my Facebook page:

Dear Lady Friends,

I need your help. What stresses you out the most? I need one-word answers.

Thanks,
Your Weird Writer Friend

Within a few minutes I had ten answers, which I dutifully noted on my yellow ledger. By bedtime I had dozens of responses, and more than eighty suggestions by the end of the next day. (Two male friends who decided to be smart alecks answered, and I threw their ideas right out. Even though they were pretty hilarious answers.) When I grouped the women's responses I found three categories: the stress of general life, the stress others cause us, and the stress we cause ourselves. These three kinds of stress have turned us into sleep-deprived zombies with churning stomachs and to-do lists three feet long. Many of my friends' suggestions make up the topics that follow, and I thank them for sharing.

As you read, I hope your spirits will lift. I pray you'll laugh out loud, possibly shooting some sort of beverage out your nose at least once. I want you to realize every other woman has her own set of angst, and God is bigger than any stress we may face.

We are not alone. We have each other as we muddle through this messy life, and our God is with us.

Our God is with us! I feel better already; do you?

Make It Personal

1. What is stressing you out right now?
2. How have you been handling the problems?
3. What changes do you want to see in yourself and in the situation?

Scripture Focus

"And as God's grace reaches more and more people, there will be great thanksgiving, and God will receive more and more glory. That is why we never give up. Though our bodies are dying, our spirits are being renewed every day. For our present troubles are small and won't last very long. Yet they produce for us a glory that vastly outweighs them and will last forever! So we don't look at the troubles we can see now; rather, we fix our gaze on things that cannot be seen. For the things we see now will soon be gone, but the things we cannot see will last forever" (2 Cor. 4:15–18).

A Prayer for Today

Heavenly Father, I'm not sure how much more stress I can take. I know these problems are small and temporary in the eternal scheme of things, but they feel enormous and permanent. I want to fix my gaze on what you find important, but I don't know how to do that. Please help me to find your peace in the midst of my circumstances. I seek your perspective instead of my own. Amen.

Part 1

The Relentless, Endless Muck of Adulthood

The Stress of General Life

I TAKE FULL responsibility for some of the stress in my life. I'm an adult, and I realize I cause my own problems half the time.

But sometimes it's not my fault. Sometimes it's not your fault either. Life happens and drags us right into it, whether we are interested or not.

Think back to when you were eight and you wanted nothing more than to be a grown-up. You couldn't wait to decide your own bedtime and scoop as much ice cream as you wanted into your own bowl. Adults had it made, and you knew it.

Except now I'm an adult and I understand why all the tall people around me rolled their eyes whenever I complained about being a kid. What child has ever had to call customer service in India to forcefully explain why she is not interested in a subscription to their company's herbal supplement program? Our credit card numbers were stolen a few months ago and I had to do exactly this. Our credit union sensed the fraud and shut down our card before too much damage occurred, but not before some goober signed me up for this herbal supplement nonsense and then had the things delivered to my house.

What kind of a person has the product shipped to the owners of the stolen card numbers? It was either a vast oversight on the thief's part, or—I strongly suspect—the company itself was to blame. I think the whole place is made up of crooks who steal credit card numbers, if the customer service rep's attitude was any indication. It took many minutes of increasing volume and force on my part before he finally relented and refunded my money.

These sorts of shenanigans did not figure into my vision of adulthood when I was a wee, uninformed child. I only saw the ice cream and the ability to get my ears pierced as many times as my lobes would allow. No one was going to be the boss of me!

It turns out this last dream has been thwarted by my unusually small earlobes. I don't have enough real estate on my ears to have all the piercings I wanted when I was eight. Probably a good thing, though. In hindsight, I probably would have whistled in the wind like my father warned me. I hate it when experience proves the man right.

I feel like I've wandered far from my point (because I most certainly have), which is that adulthood often brings inevitable stress. Things get dirty, and adults get to clean them. Money and debt are never-ending struggles, our health begins to fail somewhere around the thirty-year mark, and then—once we get the hang of being an adult—something changes and we have to find our footing all over again.

Things happen, and we have to respond. We can either let the stress overwhelm us, or we can attempt to find some sort of solid approach that keeps us sane.

I've tried the overwhelmed approach, and I'm really not a fan. My blood pressure rises and my eyelids twitch. My stomach churns and my thoughts race. It's not a pretty way to live. Let's see if together we can attack one problem at a time and find the better way. Shall we?

Why We Have Dirty Socks in Every Room

On Housework

WE HAVE DIRTY socks in every room for one simple reason: I am an old, tired woman and I am not going to waste the rest of my life picking up every stray sock hiding in the crevices of our home.

The same goes for those little plastic bowls I buy from IKEA. I could host an Easter egg hunt with those things because they're strewn all over the house, hidden in plain sight. We live two hours from the nearest IKEA, that wonderland of Scandinavian home goods, so I buy them in bulk on my annual trek. We own about fifteen and only two are in the cupboard. I bet there are at least three of them on the coffee table downstairs, one on the red end table, and only heaven knows where the rest of them are. Under this bed where I'm typing? In the bathtub? Nothing would surprise me.

I used to go around and gather them up, but now I just stand in the kitchen and yell, "Go look for the bowls!" and the kids shuffle around the house in search of their missing snack holders. They bring me piles of them with sheepish grins, hoping their childish cuteness will stall any potential lectures about remembering to bring kitchen supplies back to the kitchen.

I'll tell you a little secret. I don't even care anymore. When the kids run out of bowls for snacks they tend to eat right in the kitchen, which is what I prefer anyway. I have to vacuum fewer crumbs under the couch cushions. I win!

Do you remember the little robot M-O (for Microbe-Obliterator) from *Wall-E*? He scooted around cleaning for the entire movie. He couldn't stop himself because he was programmed to clean all the time. I fidgeted all through that movie, mostly because that silly little cartoon character hit pretty close to home. It was like watching a digital version of myself. I used to stomp around my house, picking up things without ceasing, getting angrier and angrier that no one was noticing how messy everything looked. My family found this habit endearing and charming, I'm quite sure. Because having a hysterical cleaning lady for a mother is a wonderful experience, right?

Then one day I stopped looking at perfect magazine photos and really looked around my friends' houses. It turns out that a real home includes vastly more clutter than a magazine house. (Plus dust, grime, smelly shoes, and mysterious piles of flip-flops that may or may not have owners.) I'm willing to bet magazine photographers stuff everything into a closet before they click the shutter, or no one actually lives in that room. Realizing this was the first step in my M-O recovery process.

> It turns out that a real home includes vastly more clutter than a magazine house.

But that step to recovery didn't eliminate my cleaning issues. Do you know what else stresses me out? Weird smells. I blame this on the years I was a social worker, when I often visited homes that were chaotic, messy, and obnoxiously stinky. My word, the smells! The combination of stale air, cigarette smoke, unwashed clothing, and whatever was rotting on the kitchen counter set me back a few paces. My mother comes from a long line of Polish housewives who think nothing of wiping down the baseboards weekly with boiling bleach, so I wasn't prepared for this level of non-housekeeping. I didn't actually know it was possible for a house to have so many bad odors until my short-lived career in the social services taught me otherwise.

I tell you all this to explain my current level of housekeeping, which emphasizes fresh air and a general level of tidiness, but falls far short of my great-grandmother's boiling bleach. I can either live my life or get my house spotless, but I cannot do both. I've had to decide what bothers me and what I can let slide. Dust I ignore for months. Dishes I tend to wash immediately, often before we even eat dinner. Our coffee table's continually piled with books, ear buds, and possibly the cat. I've decided it's charming like that.

Other women have different standards because what drives us crazy differs from woman to woman. I wonder how our stress levels would respond if we prioritized our cleaning according to what bothered us (and maybe our husbands, if they're the neat ones), and ignored what everyone else was saying. What freedom would we experience if we just threw the latest shelter magazine into the recycle bin and didn't even compare it to our own humble situation?

I think that might be a comfort. A blessed, although slightly dusty, comfort.

Another comfort is this: learning that life has seasons, and with those seasons come different levels of mess. Take my little friend Liam (name changed because one day he'll be old enough to read this and I still want him to like me), who was the pukiest baby I've ever met. The kid started projectile vomiting fresh out of the womb and didn't give it up for months. On Sundays when I was scheduled to serve in the nursery, I'd plan my outfit based on layers I could shed after handing him back to his mom.

I had a favorite sweater that didn't make it to church for an entire winter because I knew all Liam's spit-up would pool in the soft woolen threads, and I didn't want to destroy my five-dollar find from the thrift store. (My poor laundry skills killed off that sweater. Wool cannot survive the dryer. How old do I have to be before I remember this?) Whatever I wore needed to be washed when we got home.

But I only had the child for an hour on Sunday. Can you imagine his mother's laundry piles? The sheets, his clothes, her clothes, the baby blankets, the towels—everything needed to be washed all the time. After months and months of this, Liam's mother finally found a medical treatment that helped him. Just like that, her laundry loads dropped in half. Just like that, she regained a little bit of her sanity.

One day (if we've trained them well), the kids will stop being tornadoes of destruction, and we will regain some of our sanity too. They won't leave train tracks strewn across the entire living room. They won't splatter toothpaste all over the mirror. They'll be able to operate the washing machine all on their own, even. The house will grow quiet and tidy as they move out into their own lives and have their own children who destroy their houses. These seasons are temporary, and realizing this can be one little step into lowering our stress level.

Messy houses and piles of laundry don't mean we're bad housekeepers; they just signify that life is happening in our homes. We're riding a tidal wave of chaos and not going under. This is something we should celebrate, I think. Did your laundry pile not kill you today? Then let's put that in the "win" column.

When we celebrate and welcome the life in our homes, we're on the right track. The Bible never once tells us our value is based on how clean our tubs are or how tidily our linens are folded. But it does tell us to carefully guard the important things in our hearts and to focus on what's really important.

Jesus had some pretty strong feelings about the dangers of focusing on the outward appearances of our lives but neglecting the condition of our hearts. He stated fiercely to the hypocritical religious leaders: "You ignore the more important aspects of the law—justice, mercy, and faith. . . . What sorrow awaits you teachers of religious law and you Pharisees. Hypocrites! For you are so careful to clean the outside of the cup and the dish, but inside you are filthy—full of greed and self-indulgence! You blind Pharisee! First wash the inside of the cup and the dish, and then the outside will become clean, too" (Matt. 23:23, 25–26).

I will be the first to admit it's way easier to focus on the outward appearance of my house than the inward condition of my heart. I can fool visitors and even my family if things are tidy on the outside. I imagine them walking into the living room and thinking, "My goodness, Jessie really has it all together. She must be a super person because I see fresh vacuum tracks on the carpet."

But keeping up those appearances is stressful. The house will never be clean because we still live here, as that Pinterest meme so accurately states. It's tempting to focus on housekeeping, but so much more satisfying to focus on getting my heart right with God. Washing the inside of the cup, as Jesus said, means I'm clean where it matters. My heart can celebrate the people who live in this house, the companionship with each other we find among the stray socks, and the snacks we nibble from brightly-colored little bowls we're about to discard on the coffee table. Again.

It's not about how sanitized the baseboards are or how fresh the sheets smell. It's about a heart that worships a God who gave us houses and clothes and dishes and food. It's about creating a welcoming home where feet can shuffle around the toys and the cat can nap in the middle of the bed. It's about lives that are well lived, with hearts that joyfully receive the blessings given.

Worship, joy, and love trump a clean house any day, don't you think? I certainly do.

And if you're anywhere near an IKEA, can you buy me a package of bowls? I'd appreciate it.

Make It Personal

1. What housekeeping project is stressing you out right now? Is it something that bothers you, or something that you worry bothers other people?
2. If you could prioritize your housework based on your own preferences, what five jobs would you put at the top?
3. Jesus warned the Pharisees to attend to their hearts instead of just

outward appearances. What is one thing you could do this week to deepen your spiritual life?

Scripture Focus

"When they arrived, Samuel took one look at Eliab and thought, 'Surely this is the LORD's anointed!' But the LORD said to Samuel, 'Don't judge by his appearance or height, for I have rejected him. The LORD doesn't see things the way you see them. People judge by outward appearance, but the LORD looks at the heart'" (1 Sam. 16:6–7).

A Prayer for Today

Heavenly Father, please give me strength to handle all this housework that never seems to end. Help me to celebrate the family who shares this place with me. Help me to be thankful for what you have provided. And in all things, may I seek a heart that is right with you before I worry about the ring in that bathtub. Amen.

Cute New Shoes Will Not Fix This Mess, but It Can't Hurt to Try Them On

On finances

I ACCIDENTALLY WANDERED into Saks Fifth Avenue last weekend while we were in Indianapolis. It was a distinctly uncomfortable ten minutes as I shuffled around, fairly desperate to get out of there. For one thing, I was wearing the same clothes I'd worn to the park earlier—the same clothes I intended to wear on the four-hour drive home. I wasn't gross or indecent, but I felt like Saks might be a store where a tiara wasn't overdressing. I wasn't wearing my tiara and my five-dollar T-shirt from Target wasn't really matching the feel of the place.

Eric picked up a pair of sneakers that cost *five hundred and fifty dollars*. I think one of my eyeballs may have popped out of the socket when he told me the price with a straight face.

We'd landed in what must be Indy's most expensive mall due to my husband's new obsession with Tesla's electric vehicles. Wealthy drivers who like to be environmentally friendly, while still having the acceleration of a launching rocket, are generally the only people who can afford these things. (Certainly not our family.) Teslas aren't sold in Michigan as of this writing, so when Eric realized we were close to a showroom in a mall, he had to see these vehicles up close. Let me summarize—we started with one-hundred-thousand–dollar cars and ended with Saks Fifth Avenue, and I was wearing a five-dollar T-shirt.

As we left I muttered, "There's nothing about this mall that makes me feel good about anything happening in America right now." The area was loaded to the gills with shoppers, and I had been watching the people and wondering if anyone actually had money for all the things they were buying. Days later, I'm still wondering. If I had interviewed a hundred women in that mall, I bet I would have heard a hundred different stories about how money was affecting their lives. A few of them probably had budgets and shopped responsibly after they saved money in their retirement accounts, and a few shoppers probably could have afforded the $550 sneakers without even looking at the price tag. But other than those few souls, I'm willing to wager that a portion of the group might have cried a little during some portion of our money discussion.

That's what money does to us. It's supposed to be a neutral tool that helps us access the resources we need for daily life, but it turns into a monster that squeezes our guts with stress. We make financial choices from emotional places that rarely have anything to do with math or logic.

> We make financial choices from emotional places that rarely have anything to do with math or logic.

The woman who grew up in poverty may now use money as protection from the pain of scarcity. Her shelves bulge with overstocked clothing, food, and toilet paper. She'll never be hungry again if she has anything to say about it. Or, she might save every extra cent. There will be no fun, no giving, no luxury, until she's saved enough to weather any financial storm. This bottomless emotional pit fuels her hoarding. She will never stop saving or stocking up, because there is always *one more emergency* that could destroy her world.

The lady who has begun to feel old and bland may find herself at a makeup counter in the department store, buying everything the clerk recommends for her wrinkles, bags, dark circles, and puffiness. As long as her credit card is valid, she will try to outrun Father Time.

The mother who needs her children's adoration fills her cart with whatever whim appeals to the kids that day. Toys, sparkly socks, pools for the back yard—nothing is too extravagant if it makes her babies love her more.

These are only a few examples of why we all need a million dollars right now. We could use that magic money to fix the bad financial choices we've made, pay the bills that are piling up on the table, get that flappy skin under our belly buttons tucked back where it used to be, and then buy a car that will impress the other carpool moms. We'll be happy as clams, until the money runs out. And then we'll face an entirely new financial stress because we'll be right back where we started. No money, no peace.

Is there another way? Could we approach our money from an entirely different angle and live entirely different lives?

I'm going to be very bold and tell you there *is* another way. But it's a little frightening. It involves some reckless faith and a daily determination to include God in all of our financial decisions, attitudes, and needs. This is not for the weak-willed. The change will not be easy or fast—but it might be the only thing that pulls you out of a financial nightmare and puts you on the road to peace. Jesus said, "I am leaving you with a gift—peace of mind and heart. And the peace I give is a gift the world cannot give. So don't be troubled or afraid" (John 14:27). His peace includes all of our lives, even our financial challenges.

We serve a very personal God. He loves us and cares for us in intimate ways. In theory I know this, but I struggle with applying it to my deepest worries over money. I assume God has very big things to worry about in developing nations and war-torn lands, so probably our family's little problems here in wealthy America don't register on his radar from day to day. This is wrong, muddle-headed thinking that only leads me to depend on myself and attempt to fix my own financial problems. And basically, any time I try to fix my own problem without involving God, I dig myself into a deeper hole. I can't ensure my own financial security in this world any more than I can rotate the moon.

I'm learning to turn to God instead of looking to my own solutions, and I implore you to do the same in all aspects of your financial life. This is how we find the peace Jesus spoke about. If your finances are out of control, but you really can't understand why you're driven to spend like you do, it's okay to ask God for insight into your own behavior. What appears to be a financial problem may actually have a much deeper root cause, and prayer may be the catalyst that can give you a new understanding. If you're afraid of not having what you need, tell him that. If you feel old and dowdy and shopping temporarily makes you feel happy, ask him to help you find true joy. If you want to be a good mom and don't know how to tell your children you can't afford the stuff they want, talk to God about it.

However, your situation may have absolutely nothing to do with root psychological causes. Sometimes the situation is simply a matter of cold, hard cash. If the medical bill that arrived today is $4,209 more than you have in the checking account, report the numbers to God. Include him in every bit of your financial life and then ask him to work on your behalf. I cannot promise you that a miracle will occur and a check for $4,209 will appear in your mailbox tomorrow. God's not a genie or an ATM. Sometimes he does provide in miraculous ways, but other times his work is subtle and requires that we have a heart of faith to wait for his provision. It may come in different ways, like generous repayment terms from the hospital, an extra job, or generous gifts from friends who hear of your need.

Sometimes—and this can be terribly difficult to accept—his provision doesn't come in the way we expect. Medical bills may pile up and the good job offer may not appear. It may become a matter of trusting in his plan rather than watching a miracle unfold. Will we still seek him when the easy answer doesn't appear? Will we still praise him and trust in his goodness when his provision seems so meager? God's most intimate work in our lives may come through our finances, and sometimes that work can be exactly the opposite of what we want to experience.

Our heavenly Father can move in ways that are so much deeper than money. He can calm our deepest fears, fill the emotional voids, and teach us to value the truly important things. His ways are completely foreign to our modern financial mentality, so I'm not saying this is going to be simple. It requires letting go of a lot of beliefs and attitudes about money that may be deeply ingrained in us.

Slowly, gradually, he will create a new heart in us if we ask him to do that. Over the years I've learned I can't force a new heart for myself. But when I turn to God in submission, willing to seek him and then respond in obedience, he never leaves me where I started. Isaiah 30 gives a vision of the good life—a life that includes God's abundance—and I think it speaks strongly of our situations today. God makes his willingness to provide clear, but he also details the decisions and attitudes we must choose as we wait for his provision.

> Then the LORD will bless you with rain at planting time. There will be wonderful harvests and plenty of pastureland for your livestock. The oxen and donkeys that till the ground will eat good grain, its chaff blown away by the wind. In that day, when your enemies are slaughtered and the towers fall, there will be streams of water flowing down every mountain and hill. The moon will be as bright as the sun, and the sun will be seven times brighter—like the light of seven days in one! (Isa. 30:23–26)

I feel like a modern-day equivalent could read: "Then the Lord will bless you with regular deposits into your checking account. There will be wonderful bonuses and the exact clothing you need for the next season will always be on sale. Every resource will come effortlessly, you'll have no struggles, and endless blessing will pour into your days. Your life will be all sunshine and light, with no darkness to bother you."

This situation sounds exactly right and wonderful, doesn't it? We'd love to have God update those verses for our comfort and joy. But if there's one thing I know about the Bible, it's that we must carefully evaluate the context of any passage. It's not enough to just pull out verses and then demand that God cooperate with our quasi-biblical plans.

That's why it's important to know that passage from Isaiah was written to the Israelites who had stepped out of God's will, and he was entreating them to return to his provision and protection. They'd made a treaty with Egypt instead of relying on him. I'm not going to pretend for one little second that I'm an expert on political history, but I did find some help in *The Transforming Word: One-Volume Commentary on the Bible*. It tells us that Israel was a minor power wedged between major superpowers of the day. They tried to negotiate their own security by aligning themselves with Egypt.

"Those who trust in Yahweh have no need for Egypt," the editor comments.[1] What a wise and crucial word for us today. Israel's reliance on their political savvy brought the following comments from God. "'What sorrow awaits my rebellious children,' says the LORD. 'You make plans that are contrary to mine. You make alliances not directed by my Spirit, thus piling up your sins. For without consulting me, you have gone down to Egypt for help. You have put your trust in Pharaoh's protection. You have tried to hide in his shade'" (Isa. 30:1–2).

Whether we're an ancient minor power with menacing neighbors or a small family with empty bank accounts, we all understand the human impulse to fix our own problems. We long to know things are going to be okay. We may not be making treaties with Pharaoh, but we have new and slick ways of hiding in his proverbial shade. Things like credit cards. We tend to fill in the gaps with our Visa, an extra job, or our home equity line of credit. Or we might run to our parents' money when things get tight. Whatever we can do to make the tension go away, we try that first.

Let me be clear. There's nothing wrong with receiving money from our parents or getting an extra job. In fact, those things are often excellent financial options. It's only when we begin to rely on them instead of God that we've stepped outside his provision. When we cover our financial mess with denial, when we smooth our family problems by purchasing more useless baubles, and when we try to buy our self-esteem with anti-aging creams or expensive cars, we've turned our backs on God's way to truly solve our emotional tangles.

Would you like to know my Egypt—where I run to provide for my own security? It's dumb and I'm a little embarrassed to tell you. Every time I get nervous about our situation, I start to mentally downsize. I research every house on the market in Kalamazoo County that our family could squeeze into. The only requirements are that the mortgage drops by hundreds of dollars a month, and the taxes drop with it. Mildew in the basement? Fine. Ancient roof and 1970s kitchen? Perfect. Apparently, I prefer a wobbly toilet and bats in the attic to trusting that God can provide for us right here.

Gently, day after day, God has been showing me a better way than turning to my own solutions. Every time I stop my own plotting and pray for his provision, it comes.

Our emotional and financial security is found in God. Not in cash in our accounts, not in making our children happy, not even in a two-year supply of toilet paper stacked high in the basement. We find God by quietly coming before him and resting in him, asking for help with our very personal financial challenges.

I took some time to look over all of Isaiah 30 very carefully. This is a summary of what I hear God speaking through this passage:

Consult me.
Rest in me.
Return to me.
Wait for me.
Cry to me.
Learn from me.
Listen to me.
Look for me.
Because I am your security.

How many times does he lovingly direct our attention back to himself? I long to know what could change in our lives if we did as he asked.

That's some heart-stopping faith, right there. That's this verse, put into action: "This is what the Sovereign Lord, the Holy One of Israel, says: 'Only in returning to me and resting in me will you be saved. In quietness and confidence is your strength'" (Isa. 30:15).

But wait. There's more. It doesn't just end with our own financial and emotional peace. God's provision always flows outward, and it should flow out of us to others. Can you imagine how generous you could be if you were living from a place of financial trust? If you didn't have to protect yourself, make your kids happy, or buy expensive tubes of anti-wrinkle cream to feel good, how much would you be able to share? There's an entire world out there, literally thousands of ministries, that could directly benefit from your newfound financial peace.

> Using money to fund our own financial and emotional security is never God's way.

You might be able to pay off your debt completely, opening up hundreds of dollars a month to support your church or a ministry you love. You might even be able to change jobs to go into ministry yourself, or spend more time with your family, who desperately wants you home more often. Maybe a neighbor is barely keeping food on the table and you would have enough extra to deliver groceries until they get back on their feet. There might be a family at church that can't afford camp for their kids, but God could use your willing heart and newly available money to send those kids to a week of swimming and s'mores.

It doesn't just have to be money either. Your financial situation may not ever reach the point where you could send another family to camp. But God might bless you richly with faith, wisdom, and joy you could share with others instead. Trust me, there have been days when I've been in dire need of a joyful, wise word. It's often friends in difficult financial situations who speak the most important truth into my life. I don't need their money; I need grace from their deep connection with God.

Are you catching the vision? Is your heart pounding with the opportunities that are just waiting for you to trade a financial mess for God's provision and generosity? I promise you this is totally and absolutely possible. Using money to fund our own financial and emotional security is never God's way. There is something far better for anyone who's willing to seek God with every aspect of her financial situation.

I'll close with this verse: "So the Lord must wait for you to come to him so he can show you his love and compassion. For the Lord is a faithful God. Blessed are those who wait for his help" (Isa. 30:18). If we're willing to take God at his word, we might be moments away from a completely new kind of security, one brought by a God who can provide more than we'll ever know.

Make It Personal

1. What emotion could be fueling your financial decisions?
2. Think of one specific financial issue you could pray about this week (you have to start somewhere, and starting small is fine). Pray over the situation at least daily, but also any time it comes to mind. How do you hope the situation will change with God's involvement?

Scripture Focus

"So don't worry about these things, saying, 'What will we eat? What will we drink? What will we wear?' These things dominate the thoughts of unbelievers, but your heavenly Father already knows all your needs. Seek the Kingdom of God above all else, and live righteously, and he will give you everything you need. So don't worry about tomorrow, for tomorrow will bring its own worries. Today's trouble is enough for today" (Matt. 6:31–34).

For further study, read Isaiah 30:18–26.

A Prayer for Today

Well, Lord, I'm sure you understand our true financial situation. You know what I can see and feel from here, but you also see so far beyond my limited vision. You know what I fear, what I seek, and what will really bring me peace. Please work in my heart first, helping me to seek the kingdom above all things. I trust your ability to glorify yourself through our financial situation. Help me to turn to you and rest. Amen.

When a Sandwich from the Gas Station Deli Begins to Look Delicious

On Health

I ALWAYS BECOME a simmering ball of resentment in the dumbest places. For example, the gas station deli. I barely even go into gas stations because they creep me out, but when I do, I'm often hungry and crabby and in the mood to eat something terrible. I see the plastic-wrapped sandwiches in the cooler and then I suddenly grow furious because I can't eat one. Yes, you understand me correctly—I become enraged when I'm denied a dried-out, questionable sandwich from the QuikMart.

Hangry. It's a thing. Part hungry, part angry, all me.

Never mind that my husband claims one of the best sandwiches he's ever had in his life came from a gas station. That station happened to be in Tuscany, where they suffer no bad food. Not even at the rest stop on the A1 Motorway, headed north toward Florence. The Italians aren't going to put up with gummy cheese or dried-out bread, even if it's only for a quick stop for fuel and a snack.

I couldn't enjoy a fabulous sandwich there, thanks to my celiac disease. I was diagnosed in my early thirties with an autoimmune disorder that can only be managed with a gluten-free diet. I have to stick to the diet religiously—no cheating ever, because the side effects of sneaking wheat are wide and unpleasant. So if you suffer under the delusion that only hipsters wearing organic cotton pants eat that gluten-free stuff, let me disabuse you of that notion. There are also a few of us out there with a genuine medical issue.

As much as I'd like to eat normal sandwiches, Twinkies, or Costco pizza (my life goals are terribly mediocre), I'm pretty lucky compared to my friend with Crohn's disease. It requires her to get monthly infusions of a frightening drug that shuts off her immune system. And compared to my other friend who is losing her fingernails from her cancer treatments, I should be falling on my knees in thankfulness.

Health problems. They stress us out because there's a lot of fear involved in illness. What if I can't take care of my family? What if I can't work and we fall behind on the bills? What if this lump is a serious problem? Let us not forget our children's health problems, which cause an entirely different type of stress. Thanks to the miracle of the internet, we can be terrified of every sniffle and headache, certain the kids have been infected with a terminal illness. And, of course, all of us know a family where those silly fears became a stark reality. We just don't know how we'd make it through.

Even if we're all fine, sometimes the most insidious stress is waiting for the worst to happen, borrowing trouble before its time. Every time a body gives out on us or might possibly give out on us, it feels like we're missing our chance to live life to the full.

I don't know about your family specifically, but our house screeches to a halt when I get sick. Everything falls apart. If I'm not bustling around this joint, keeping everything moving, chaos swallows us whole. I lie down and close my eyes for a few minutes, and I wake up to Legos strewn across three rooms, cat hair dusting all the surfaces, something burning in the oven, and children battling in the far reaches of the house. We want to take care of our people, and being healthy is a crucial step of that caring. Life only feels right when we're on the move. We'll do anything to avoid an illness-induced slowdown.

On the Fourth of July, a group of us were sitting around on our friends' back deck. We'd just eaten a large lunch and were waiting for it to settle so we could begin our large dinner. (We celebrate America's independence with food, okay?) While our digestive systems chugged along, Dwight decided we could use the time wisely to plan out this book. I rambled through some of the chapter topics and his eyes lit up when I mentioned this chapter.

"You should talk about how women take all their little symptoms to the internet to diagnose themselves, even when it's nothing. But when it comes to really big things, they pretend it's not worth a trip to the doctor."

I blinked at him and pretended not to know what he was talking about. Because I've never, ever (cough, cough) done that. "I need more information," I said.

"Jane was feeling a little pain in her chest here and there. She mentioned it a few times but didn't get to the doctor. One night she said, 'Honey, I really don't feel well. I think we should go in.' So I took her to the emergency room, but they weren't paying any attention to us . . ."

(Now here we have to pause while I give a little public service announcement. I don't recommend what Dwight did next, but he did it and it's part of the story. I don't want you trying it and then having your angry doctor calling my house to yell at me. So take this as information, not a recommendation. We now return to Dwight and our regularly scheduled programming.)

". . . and I didn't want to sit there all night for nothing. So I told them I thought she might be having a heart attack. That got their attention! Turned out she had a pulmonary embolism."

Jane's fine now. Everything's fine. But that's exactly the sort of thing we women do sometimes—chug through our days, sick and sicker, until we end up in the ER with the husband telling fibs to the medical staff. We have a hard time showing ourselves the kindness we show to the rest of the family. Rest and recovery are for other people, not for us.

But we shouldn't think taking care of ourselves is selfish, right? It may feel that way, but we're of no use to anyone when we finally drop on the ground from exhaustion, anemia, a pulmonary embolism, or whatever other disease might be chasing us down. We're actually taking care of others when we take care of ourselves.

> We're actually taking care of others when we take care of ourselves.

Sometimes we're not refusing to acknowledge our human limitations, though. Sometimes we're just furious because our bodies have failed us and we deeply resent being forced to make changes. We may hate the diabetic diet or the wheelchair or the unending medical appointments. But what we're really livid about is the interruption to our lives.

Hey, I completely understand. I've been in tears over ice cream when I found pieces of brownie lurking beneath the surface. I had to throw the entire cup away or suffer explosive diarrhea the next day. What kind of choice is that? It's dumb and aggravating. I can only imagine what it would feel like to have legs that don't work, or to spend an entire day throwing up because of chemo treatments.

We know sickness isn't part of God's original plan. We tend to think of it as an evil. We resist and fight it, assuming it's blocking us from living our true life and calling. But what if God is working deeply through our health problems? What if this is something he allows because it will do the deepest work in our hearts? Our fullest life might actually come through this struggle.

Let me share something with you. I read this recently in *Walking on Water* by Madeleine L'Engle. She is speaking to writers and other creative types:

> Wounds. By his wounds we are healed. But they are our wounds, too, and until we have been healed we do not know what wholeness is. The discipline of creation, be it to paint, compose, write, is an effort toward wholeness.
>
> The great male artists have somehow or other retained this

wholeness, this being in touch with both intellect and intuition, a wholeness which always has to be bought at a price in this world. How many artists, in the eyes of the world, have been less than whole? Toulouse-Lautrec had the body of a man and the legs of a child. Byron had a clubfoot. Demosthenes was a terrible stutterer. Traditionally, Homer was blind. The great artists have gained their wholeness through their wounds, their epilepsies, tuberculoses, periods of madness.[2]

L'Engle is suggesting that our fullest life might actually come through struggle, and further, that our greatest contribution to the *world* might come through it too. Like Christ, in fact. She references 1 Peter 2:24; here is the whole passage of Scripture.

For God called you to do good, even if it means suffering, just as Christ suffered for you. He is your example, and you must follow in his steps. He never sinned, nor ever deceived anyone. He did not retaliate when he was insulted, nor threaten revenge when he suffered. He left his case in the hands of God, who always judges fairly. He personally carried our sins in his body on the cross so that we can be dead to sin and live for what is right. By his wounds you are healed. Once you were like sheep who wandered away. But now you have turned to your Shepherd, the Guardian of your souls. (1 Peter 2:21–25)

By his wounds I am healed, Peter says. But I don't feel healed when I sit with my pitiful gluten-free sandwich. Do you know what gluten-free bread tastes like? Like Styrofoam flour held together with tears and sadness. I still feel sick, set apart, and unable to partake in life around me.

Maybe you don't feel Christ's healing as you sit in the doctor's chair, connected to the IVs that bring Lyme disease treatment but suck your bank account dry. Maybe you don't feel healed as you wait for your checkup each year, fully aware the cancer could be back.

And yet, I believe the Bible to be true. So perhaps the healing Christ brings is more than just healing of our bones and cells. Maybe he's speaking of wholeness that goes further than our bodies, deep to the quiet parts of our souls.

Certainly, Christ healed physical ailments. Some of the most breath-taking stories in the Gospels involve Jesus stopping in his tracks to mend a body—the bleeding woman, the leper, Peter's mother-in-law. We want that healing, that same gentle touch. We want to know he sees our brokenness and will come near to make us whole again. But Peter just told us—he brought us wholeness on the cross, with his own broken body.

Our bodies may be broken, but Jesus was broken too. For us.

May I be perfectly honest? I don't know how my suffering helps me or anyone else. I don't even completely understand how Jesus's suffer-ing heals anyone. I don't know, really and truly, how it even helps me. Why did Christ have to suffer to bring us healing? I don't see the link between his suffering and my suffering and the rest of the world. It seems mysterious and godly and totally beyond my understanding.

Do you know what's fascinating and terribly important about this passage from Peter? It's in the middle of many passages about submis-sion to authority. Citizens are reminded to submit to authorities, slaves are taught to accept their masters' directions, Christ-followers are called to submit like Christ, and husbands and wives are called to submit to each other. And we, as a church, are called to humbleness and love.

I want to push away my medical diagnosis, but maybe it's submission that will bring me healing and deliver me to my potential. While here, on this broken planet, we are called to spiritual submission to a God who could heal our bodies in an instant if he chooses. Of course we continue to pray for healing, in complete faith that he can do it. But as we wait, we submit and look for the kind of healing that will never show up in a lab report. Wholeness that a medical doctor will never find with a stethoscope.

It's entirely possible I'll spend the rest of my days denied a dried-out, gummy sandwich from the QuikMart. But do you know where I'd be without my diagnosis, the iron tablets, and the multivitamins? Possibly dead. Definitely too sick to enjoy life. Complete bodily healing may not come for me, but in the meantime I'll enjoy the yogurt and salami sticks, and lo, even the gluten-free Oreo-ish cookies available at the grocery store. I'll be thankful for what healing I have, while I wait for the permanent healing to come.

Make It Personal

1. Let's have a deeply philosophical debate. How much do suffering and illness contribute to the world? Do they grow anything good? Do they produce bad? How?
2. If you or a loved one suffers from illness, what benefits have you seen?

Scripture Focus

"The LORD is my shepherd; I have all that I need. He lets me rest in green meadows; he leads me beside peaceful streams. He renews my strength. He guides me along right paths, bringing honor to his name. Even when I walk through the darkest valley, I will not be afraid, for you are close beside me. Your rod and your staff protect and comfort me" (Ps. 23:1–4).

A Prayer for Today

Heavenly Father, I'm sick. I can't get anything done, the house is a wreck, and the medical bills are piling up. I don't feel like this is your plan for abundant life. I pray in faith for your healing. But if you don't choose to heal me, I pray for the grace to accept your decision. If there's anything good that can come out of this, I pray you'll help me see it. Please calm my fears over my health and my children's health. I know sometimes I worry about things before they're even a reality. Help me to rest in you, no matter what comes. Amen.

I Demand an Explanation for All This Extra Skin

On Aging

I'M SURE THE reading public assumes writers wake up from their slumber, jolt out of bed, and then scurry to their laptops to capture the inspiration from their dreams.

This is not how it happens.

How it happens is this: I know I need to write, but I'm afraid of actually writing, so I spend at least thirty minutes procrastinating. I usually start at least one load of laundry and might sweep the kitchen floor. Since I'm in the kitchen I may as well get a snack, and since I'm nervous about writing, it will need to be especially delicious to calm my nerves. Today's selection included Nestle chocolate chunks that will never make it into a cookie recipe, and potato chips with some dip. A little too much dip, to be honest.

Now I'm sitting down to write and my guts are churning, because what else would they do with a combination of chocolate chunks, fried potatoes, and sour cream? When I was younger I could eat everything and never feel anything but full. There was no gut pain. There was no heartburn.

Now I'm at my laptop with antacid on my breath. This is how writers actually work.

The digestive issues probably tie into the celiac disease. But mostly it's because I'm getting older. I'm forty years old, and I've accumulated four decades of scars, varicose veins, and injuries. I'm lucky I can rise from my bed in the morning with all this deterioration.

And listen. I eat well (if one ignores the recent snack selections). I exercise. Can someone please explain what the heck is happening to my body? Why does it feel the need to suddenly, after a lifetime of tucking excess fat into my butt, also grow a fluffy addition right under my belly button? What is going on here? I swear to you—this new fat is actually trying to recline on my lap at this very moment. I keep picking it up to move it elsewhere, but there's nowhere for it to go!

(If you are a man, I must insist that you skip a few paragraphs ahead at this point because you are simply not allowed to read this part. First of all, what is a man doing reading this book anyway? I don't know anything about men and stress. It seems to involve a lot of yelling and throwing things in the garage. Please go away and throw something in the garage and leave us ladies in peace while we discuss boobs.)

Yes, boobs. I used to have them. They are slowly melting, possibly into that pooch of fat that rests on my lap. Right now it looks like my breasts are youthful and firm, and that is one-hundred-percent due to the bra I'm wearing. I could give the table next to me a solid set of B cups if I put the bra on it. My boobs themselves are just pitiful sacks of cells, limp and squishy. I miss them.

Come back, dear bosom. You are missed.

(Men, you may now rejoin the conversation if you are so inclined.)

We will not discuss what is happening to the underside of my arms. I can't even find the words to discuss this problem area, and I don't have time to cry for an hour. Let's just move along. But if someone wants to invent a bra for upper arms, I will buy that thing. In all the colors.

With all these body issues, it's amazing women don't just shut themselves into a dark room and live out the last three decades of life covered in gauzy death gowns. Who can bear our hideousness? But somehow we manage to soldier on, going out in public and even—horror of horrors—wearing sleeveless tanks. Shorts! Skirts! High heels!

None of us have time to slowly vanish beneath the weight of our death gowns. We have things to do and people to love and careers to manage. Puffy bellies, wrinkly faces, and all. We carry on, and in doing so, we're examples to the other women around us. I think my friends would be nervous if they knew how much I watch them live. It's how I daily figure out how to do this thing called life. I watch Susanne and Kara for ideas on how to eat healthfully and exercise. I watch Linda as she mentors the young girls in her church. I watch how Caron, Becky, and Louise take care of their husbands as they move through their elderly years. I'm watching, watching, watching. I may be growing older, but I'm thankful to be doing it with good company. The physical changes don't matter as much when I see how my friends are moving gracefully through their years. A few wrinkles and gray hairs don't matter much when I also see the deep and caring relationships they've built.

> I think my friends would be nervous if they knew how much I watch them live.

At the same time, I get to be an example for my younger friends who are just starting to figure out adulthood. God, in his infinite sense of humor, has placed Eric and me in a small group at church that's full of young families. Eric and I weren't exactly poster children for the Young Family Movement. We had our two kids and, while I was still on the operating table from Caleb's cesarean, I had some surgical intervention to derail the Clemence Baby Train. We bore down and gritted our teeth and barely survived those baby and toddler years. Of course we loved our kids, but we really didn't love the experience of parenting tiny children. And now we're in a small group that's loaded to the gills with that exact type of human.

There are times when we're in small group and the young mothers are talking about their day, and I just want to weep for them. Kimmy's baby threw up in her mouth yesterday. IN HER MOUTH. Elisabeth is four feet, ten inches tall and she's six months pregnant. There's no place for that baby to go. The woman is all fetus, with three months left to gestate. I fear the baby will swallow her alive. Ellie can't get a thing done without her son John "helping" her. Katherine is trying to take classes and care for a two-year-old. Tish is trying to stop her one-year-old from climbing up and falling down every set of steps in Kalamazoo County.

These precious women are telling me these exhausting stories, and all I can say is, "I'm sorry. I'm sorry. I'm so, so sorry." We asked another couple to join the group, somewhat out of desperation. Mark and Catherine are about a decade older than us, and they swooped into our group with their gentle spirits and just set the whole thing straight. You've never met more loving, caring people than those two, and they breathe grace into us all. They've made wise financial choices, parented their kids with excellence through really difficult situations, and have loved our church for decades. We constantly have an eye on them, watching and learning how they've gotten from there to here. They have the right priorities, and they prayerfully work their way to God's best in every area of their life.

I have literally seen Kimmy's three-year-old marching around my house wearing Catherine's diamond necklace. I had visions of my vacuum sucking up the family's heirloom jewels if Ruby lost them.

"Yikes, Catherine. You're brave to let Ruby wear your jewelry!" I said.

She just shrugged and—I am not making this up—said, "They're just things. It doesn't matter." Mark sat next to her, smiling benevolently, like his wife handed diamonds to toddlers every day. Maybe she does. Maybe they have a stash of diamonds just for toddlers.

I'm not saying that jewels have to be involved as we invest in other women, but I do know we are called to invest. Even if our only contribution to the conversation is to grab our friend by the hand and say, "I remember. I remember how terribly hard it was. You're doing fine." Someone needs to speak some words of grace and encouragement into the younger generation. And God has given you the experience to do it. Remember all those tantrums you survived as your toddler threw herself on the floor in the grocery store? The fight you had with your husband that lasted two weeks? The time you moved across the country and had to make a whole new life? Somewhere right around you, a younger woman might need to hear how you survived and how she can too.

Titus 2:3–5 says, "Similarly, teach the older women to live in a way that honors God. They must not slander others or be heavy drinkers. Instead, they should teach others what is good. These older women must train the younger women to love their husbands and their children, to live wisely and be pure, to work in their homes, to do good, and to be submissive to their husbands. Then they will not bring shame on the word of God."

I doubt Paul had a formal training program in mind. I bet he was watching the normal progression of the women in his life as they cared for one another. And a woman doesn't have to be ninety-eight to have wisdom to share either. I'm an encourager to the women who are just now entering the stage I outgrew about five minutes ago. College girls can speak truth and encouragement to the high school girls. And all of us can teach the toddlers how to properly accessorize their sunglasses to their flip flops, right? We all have some expertise to share.

Mostly what our friends need isn't expertise, anyway. Experts get annoying. What we need are companions and fellow travelers. We need someone to laugh (or cry) when we tell the story about the baby throwing up on us again. We need someone to grab our two-year-old and get clothes back on him when our hands are full with the baby, and we need someone who will encourage us through our marriage troubles. We need women who can pray for us and remind us to look to God in all situations.

We weren't made to walk this life alone, and frankly, men aren't always the best companions when it comes to some portions of our lives. It *appears* they're right next to us, experiencing the same thing, but we all know they're not actually experiencing the same thing. I don't know what's going on in those testosterone-soaked heads of theirs, but it resembles nothing that's going on in this estrogen-loaded crazy town between my ears.

I need other women to help me live my life well. Kind, generous, funny, honest women. I don't care if they have extra skin. I don't care if they don't have abs like a twenty-year-old athlete. I just want them to be focused on the right thing so I can figure out what the right thing is too. Too many women have been led astray into the wrong things, and I see the wreckage of their lives. I want to avoid that wreckage.

Show me how, my sisters. Show me how to do this. And I will do the same for others.

Make It Personal

1. Whatever your stage in life is right now, who is teaching you? Are you learning from the good example they've presented, or are you trying to avoid the wreckage they're enduring?
2. Who can you invest in? Who needs your encouragement and companionship?

Scripture Focus

"Two people are better off than one, for they can help each other succeed. If one person falls, the other can reach out and help. But someone who falls alone is in real trouble. Likewise, two people lying close together can keep each other warm. But how can one be warm alone? A person standing alone can be attacked and defeated, but two can stand back-to-back and conquer. Three are even better, for a triple-braided cord is not easily broken" (Eccl. 4:9–12).

A Prayer for Today

Heavenly Father, there are days I feel off track and destined for doom. Please help me to find older women who can show me the right things, and give me a heart that seeks the right things too. May I also be a loving friend to those who are coming up behind me. May I not be a bossy know-it-all, but a gentle example. Amen.

Kissing and Other Mushy Problems

On Romance

I ALWAYS PROMISE myself that I won't write about sex, but here I am again. Writing about sex. And kissing. And mushy stuff. As much as I'd like to sidestep this conversation, we have to address it because romance can be a major cause of stress. And a lack of it is stressful too. I can tell you one thing: there is no such thing as a trouble-free romantic life. It's a lot of work, whether you're hunting up a spouse or trying to live with the one you found.

One of the things I find most stressful about marriage is that no matter how long a couple has been together, it's quite likely everything's about to change. This spring our small group did a marriage study together. The study had a different topic every week, and Eric and I were in the nursery watching all the babies on the sex discussion night. There's some irony there, but I'm not exactly sure what it is.

So we missed most of the conversation, but as we brought the babies back to their parents at the end of the evening, we caught the last crucial conversation. These young parents were openly mocking those individuals who have premarital sex to "ensure sexual compatibility."

One of our small group members said, "If you think that sex after marriage, after babies, is anything like sex before marriage, then you're crazy." (We're not going to touch on the obvious question of how he knew anything about sex before marriage.)

His point was this—sexual compatibility is a constant effort. It's a constant relearning of everything you thought you knew. If a person thinks the emotions and physical sensations they feel in the first months of a relationship bear any resemblance to the emotions and physical needs of a woman who has a two-month-old baby, that person is an idiot.

> One of the things I find most stressful about marriage is that no matter how long a couple has been together, it's quite likely everything's about to change.

In the early days of the relationship the rush of excitement carries you through, especially if you've been waiting for a long time to find the right person. After you've been married a while, the excitement wears off and some of the physical chemistry naturally disappears with it. But that's nothing compared to the issues that develop the first months after a child has been born. Let's not get too graphic about it, but the very spots that used to be prime real estate in the whoopee department are now completely repurposed. There's leaking and swelling and pain and that's the exact opposite of sexy.

Not to mention that you and your spouse, that very man who used to chase you around the house to make sweet, sweet love to you (I can't believe I typed that either), is now simply another soldier in the trenches. The two of you are trying to keep this tiny, screeching creature alive at the exact times you used to spend two hours in foreplay. Now you'd trade an arm for two hours of sleep with no one touching you. No one at all.

Fast-forward a few years. Your body has healed up and your kids are old enough to actually sleep. Hopefully your sex life has recovered, although this will not happen without a lot of effort and caring and understanding from both partners. You get the hang of it again, even though this new sex is often burdened with heavy work schedules and endless responsibilities. But things are okay, at least until you hit middle age, and then your body starts acting up in all kinds of unspeakable ways. Again, I won't get too graphic here, but go find a book about perimenopause and then apply all those symptoms to your downstairs privacy.

That's what one of our kids called their private parts one day. We about died laughing.

Anyway, sex and downstairs privacies are only two of the ways our relationships change. There are lots of nonphysical issues as well. Husbands make mistakes. Sometimes they buy dumb things. They cheat sometimes, and sometimes we do too. They might get new jobs in places we don't want to move, or they might get sick. They might get Alzheimer's. And sometimes they die when you least expect it.

It's all a constant effort, a constant relearning.

Even long-time, established relationships hit rocky patches. Sometimes out of the blue. I recently heard a story of an older couple who had been married for decades. They had adult children. Things were good and stable for many years, but then, without warning or explanation, the husband suddenly became obsessed with a new hobby that shook their marriage to the core.

He started to spend all his waking hours committed to his new interest, and one day the wife came home and found a note that he'd gone on vacation with other aficionados. He took a lot of their money for his trip.

I'd like to tell you that after some therapy, everything was okay. But it's not okay. They divorced. The wife was going through old photos with her kids recently, and she had no choice but to see the pictures from their early family years. "I looked at him in the pictures and thought, 'Where did you go?' I remember that man, but I don't know where he went," she said.

I think a lot of us can relate. *Where did you go? Where did I go?* The love, or what we thought was love, has turned to dust in our hands or at least morphed into something we barely recognize.

All of us are tempted to lose hope, aren't we? What we can see and feel right now seems endless. No relief in sight. We're tempted to take matters into our own hands. But wait. Before we do that, can we please take a moment to refocus our attention from the problem to the work the Holy Spirit may want to do in our hearts? I don't mean to demean your experience even the tiniest little bit. I truly don't. I know your pain is real and deep; you're not a middle school student with flailing emotions. This burden is intense.

But it is sometimes in the middle of those endless burdens that the Holy Spirit can do the deepest work on our behalf. When I have given up hope, this seems to be exactly when he comes in and changes everything. The situation, maybe not, but my heart—yes. Where I have lost hope, he restores it. Where I am angry and aggravated, he shows me the truth about my circumstances and myself. He changes *me*.

None of this happens if I keep my focus on the problem. I can choose the same emotions and the same decisions, and get the same angry, worn-out results. Or I can choose differently. My life doesn't have to look like this. My marriage doesn't have to look like this. My emotions don't have to be shot, worn down, and exasperated like this. I get to choose.

And you do too.

My pastor is preaching through the entire book of 1 Corinthians, and it has taken us months and months to get to the Love Chapter. This verse convicted me and about set my hair on fire last week in the sermon. "Love never gives up, never loses faith, is always hopeful, and endures through every circumstance" (1 Cor. 13:7). That's love, friends. That's where romance lives.

I've never lost hope for my marriage, but I have another relationship where I am well past hope. I see no evidence of this other person changing. The situation isn't going to change either. I've written the whole thing off as a mess and washed my hands of it. I can't imagine it ever getting better. So, while my marriage might not be my issue, I certainly can relate with some of the struggle. I know what it's like to want to erase all connections and move out of state and permanently remove a person's chair from the table.

But God's Word shows us a different way. The way that doesn't give up, lose hope, or peter out before the race is over. Faith may move the mountains, but it's love that makes that move worthwhile. This cannot come from our limited human abilities. Don't think for a second that I'm telling you to just fix yourself and dig around in your soul and mercilessly unearth the love that's hiding in the dirt.

No, I'm speaking of the love we have because he loved us first. I'm speaking of the love that John talked about when he said, "We know how much God loves us, and we have put our trust in his love. God is love, and all who live in love live in God, and God lives in them. And as we live in God, our love grows more perfect. So we will not be afraid on the day of judgment, but we can face him with confidence because we live like Jesus here in this world" (1 John 4:16–17).

This is the only kind of love that can overcome the unending problems we face in our relationships. It's the only thing deep enough to comfort the lonely soul who cries at night. It's the kind of love Jesus had, which always found value in others. It's the kind of love that took him to the cross, completely focused on God's glory and our eternal home with him. The kind of love that chose differently, with the Holy Spirit's help.

"And we know he lives in us because the Spirit he gave us lives in us," John tells us in 1 John 3:24. That's the power we have to love truly, deeply, and beyond all human circumstances. I'd like to promise fluffy unicorns who show up right now, fixing all the problems. Your husband will bring home flowers tonight, you won't fight over who has to give the kids baths, and then you'll fall passionately into each other's arms after the kids go to bed. Poof! All your problems are solved, my friend!

We're grown-ups. We know this isn't true. Twelve months from now all of us are going to be in a completely new place in our relationships. Change is inevitable. I'm confident that in twelve months we can be stronger women if we truly peel our eyes off the problem and seek the

Holy Spirit's help to love our way through the situation like Jesus did. The situation might not change, but we will not be the same.

Does that sound ultra-holy and trite? Like something an old married lady would say when she has zero problems but a truckload of terrible advice? I hope not. I want it to sound like Paul's prayer in Ephesians 1:18–20 when he said, "I pray that your hearts will be flooded with light so that you can understand the confident hope he has given to those he called—his holy people who are his rich and glorious inheritance. I also pray that you will understand the incredible greatness of God's power for us who believe him. This is the same mighty power that raised Christ from the dead and seated him in the place of honor at God's right hand in the heavenly realms."

What would our love lives look like if the same mighty power that raised Christ from the dead took over? I can't even imagine. It would be amazing. It would probably come close to how Beverly cares for her aging husband as Alzheimer's disease turns him into a different person. And it might look like forgiveness and a smile over the kitchen table, instead of starting another fight. It might look like choosing to wear the pretty pajamas to bed instead of the enormous, ratty, stretched out blue T-shirt with the fat man wielding a sword on it. You know, the one you've had for eighteen years? (Do not pretend like you don't know what I'm talking about, my friend. Yours might not be blue, but you have one.)

It might look like hope, is all I'm saying. The brave, deep breath of hope that looks to God for patience and endurance.

Love never loses hope, the Word tells us. Let's live like that's true.

Make It Personal

1. Do you spend a lot of time fantasizing about how different your love life could look? What do you want to be different?
2. Where have you lost hope in your romantic life? How do you feel about that right now?

Scripture Focus

"Dear friends, let us continue to love one another, for love comes from God. Anyone who loves is a child of God and knows God. But anyone who does not love does not know God, for God is love. God showed how much he loved us by sending his one and only Son into the world so that we might have eternal life through him. This is real love—not that we loved God, but that he loved us and sent his Son as a sacrifice to take away our sins" (1 John 4:7–10).

A Prayer for Today

Heavenly Father, this prayer might take a long time, and there might be some crying involved. Real love, from you, looks nothing like what my hormones demand or what the world shows me. I need your help in this area: _____. Please give me your hope. May the Spirit fill in where I lack. Amen.

I Have Signed All the Consent Forms. Now I Feel Sad. And Old.

On Responsibilities

I JUST CLEANED my toilet.

After I worked half a day, wrote half a day, ran my children all over the county, made dinner, cleaned up dinner, and then started tomorrow's dinner, I cleaned my toilet.

My life is very glamorous and also sparkly.

Halfway through the pile of dinner dishes, an email dinged into my phone. It was the kids' camp, sending me special consent forms to sign so the kids can play paintball and flop around on inflatables while they're gone next week. It's like they knew I was about to sit down and write this chapter, titled "I Have Signed All the Consent Forms."

Well, technically I haven't signed those forms yet. They're still waiting for the printing and the signing. But I will get to them eventually, I promise.

I feel very adult today. I blithely signed all kinds of things. Work checks, personal checks, credit card receipts. Plus a few more things, probably. I can't even remember. My life is a haze of grown-up responsibilities.

Do you know what I fantasize about sometimes? I imagine a world where I just drop it all and walk out the door. I take my people with me, but I dump all the other things. I stop paying the mortgage and cleaning the toilet. I don't go to work. I don't mow the lawn, or make sure my children floss, or put on pants. Whether or not anyone in this house wears pants will be totally up to personal choice.

In this new miracle life, I only own yoga pants. I live in Disney World and the Dwarves bring me dinner. It is glorious. No overdue library books, no worries about my kids' grades or occupational futures, no need to vacuum the baseboards in my house. Just stretchy pants, magic dinners, a staff to clean toilets, and an occasional ride on a roller coaster.

Do you know what I'm really looking for? Joy. Fun. Delight, even. I could use a little more joy in my life. Could you? We all have to wade through the muck of adulthood, but we don't have to only wade through the muck. Sometimes we get to run and jump and splash in the fun too.

Let's reclaim joy.

A copy of *Real Simple* magazine arrived in my mailbox recently, full of summer recipes and beach cosmetics. (Its website promises quick solutions, lessons in how to do almost anything, and how to keep track of your "to-dos." Like anyone could keep track of my list.) Among the fluffy desserts and peachy drinks, an article made me open my eyes wide and say, "Yes. This is exactly right." The writer, novelist Ann Leary, had kids who were finally both headed to college. After they dropped their youngest off for the first time, she and her husband had to stop the car so they could both sob in the front seat. With puffy, bleary eyes, they made their way home and began to make dinner.

That quiet dinner was the first time in twenty years they watched TV as they ate. Leary reported that was exactly when the fun began.

They'd spent the last two decades doing every responsible thing imaginable for the good of their children. They'd stopped swearing, gossiping, and eating with their fingers. But suddenly there were no children around, no lessons to be taught. There were no morals to pass along, no table manners to enforce.

One day Leary found herself slinking to the dryer in her underwear to get some clean clothes. She says, "After I did my usual red-faced dash to the dryer, I stopped. Why was I being stealthy? The people who reacted to my body with retching sounds were gone. The one who liked me in my underwear was charging up the stairs to get a closer look."[3]

It got even better from there. She reports they began to walk around the house in nothing but their skin suits. They made love wherever and whenever they wanted, danced and sang with wild abandon, and stopped monitoring every word out of their mouths.

They rediscovered delight. They traded their responsibilities—albeit in a limited and mature fashion—for a little bit of fun. I'm pretty sure they kept working and paying the kids' tuition, but they made the whole process a lot more delightful.

After reading the article, I decided to give it a try. Right where I was. Right away. I went for my usual evening walk, but I made sure to savor the experience. I listened for the birds' late evening tweets, and I laughed at the ridiculously fluffy dog who pretended to be vicious. My son caught up with me on his bike, and together we admired the pink, purple, and orange clouds in the sky as the sun melted into the western tree line. A few brave lightning bugs started their rounds early, and I watched them pop in and out of sight. A doorless, jacked-up Jeep drove by, and the driver, an old man wearing orthotic shoes, had a foot stuck out the gap. He rested his old man shoe on the running board of his grown-up boy toy as he drove past our subdivision.

It was the same walk I take hundreds of times a year because I am a responsible human who doesn't want to gain thirty pounds this year. But it was different because I took the time to notice all the things God had put right there with me. Delight is everywhere, if we take the time to look for it. Take the time to savor it, even.

I think this pleases God. He made all these beautiful, wonderful things. But we're too busy being diligent and responsible to enjoy them. Jesus could have come to earth and walked around with a serious face all the time, but that's not what we see in the Gospels. They show us a man who enjoyed weddings and fresh-caught fish. He told stories instead of handing out heavy rulebooks. He napped on boats and took time to really get to know his friends. Jesus didn't have anything to prove by being serious all the time; he just loved people and guided them to the truth.

Why do we feel like we have so much to prove, if even Jesus knew how to relax and enjoy life? Let's follow his lead and take off the Serious Pants for a few moments. Let's replace them with the stretchy standby (or even a kicky summer dress) and find some things to enjoy.

I don't think all these good things are put here only for our enjoyment, though. I think they're put here to remind us to worship. The fun, excitement, and delight should lead us straight to God himself. Our glorious, all-powerful, almighty God saw fit to place us on this earth he has filled with fat baby thighs and wrinkly old lady faces and trees and goats. He gave us fresh breezes and thunderstorms, and all of it reflects directly on how wonderful he is.

> Our glorious, all-powerful, almighty God saw fit to place us on this earth he has filled with fat baby thighs and wrinkly old lady faces and trees and goats.

Let's take some time, in the middle of this very grown-up and official day, to think a little less of ourselves and so much more of him. Let's join the Psalmist when we say, "Praise the LORD! Praise God in his sanctuary; praise him in his mighty heaven! Praise him for his mighty works; praise his unequaled greatness! Praise him with a blast of the ram's horn; praise him with the lyre and harp! Praise him with the tambourine and dancing; praise him with strings and flutes! Praise him with a clash of cymbals; praise him with loud clanging cymbals. Let everything that breathes sing praises to the LORD! Praise the LORD!" (Ps. 150).

I love how it notes the cymbals twice—we're supposed to praise with a clash and loud clanging. That's awesome. That's a musician who's totally dedicated to a lot of loud, boisterous praising. All in, that guy.

Let's be all in too: Lord, we praise you for hot summer days and fresh sweet corn! We thank you for the changing of the seasons. We thank you for good books and delicious, fruity drinks. We thank you for cherry cobbler. We'd thank you with a double clash on the cymbals, but we don't have those handy, so we thank you by waving our phones in the air. You are just the best.

I'm going to try to keep that fun and worship going next week when both kids are at camp. It's nothing like the Learys dropping their kids off at school for months, but this will be the first time Eric and I will be home without them for this many days. We have plans for the entire week. We're going to all the places the kids hate, the places where their whining makes us regret bringing them.

This list is very long and we don't have time for the entire thing, but suffice it to say that we have a lot of things packed into next week's schedule. So many things. We plan to enjoy every minute of it, yes. But I also hope to remember to worship in the middle of it. I will be in awe of a God who made marriage and kindness and fun. I'll thank him for Lake Michigan, holding hands, and glorious sunsets.

I would not recommend stopping by unannounced either. There's a very good chance we'll follow the Learys' lead and not be entirely clothed. Consider yourself warned.

Make It Personal

1. Close your eyes and savor right where you are. What do you smell, feel, and hear?
2. What is one activity you can change today? Let's take something very responsible, like bathing the baby or mowing the lawn, and turn it into a time to worship. It might not work out, because bathing a baby is really hard, but that's okay. Try again with something different tomorrow.

Scripture Focus

"So I decided there is nothing better than to enjoy food and drink and to find satisfaction in work. Then I realized that these pleasures are from the hand of God. For who can eat or enjoy anything apart from him? God gives wisdom, knowledge, and joy to those who please him. But if a sinner becomes wealthy, God takes the wealth away and gives it to those who please him. This, too, is meaningless—like chasing the wind" (Eccl. 2:24–26).

A Prayer for Today

Father, I don't take enough time to enjoy the things you've given me. I thank you for it all. May I not be content to simply notice and appreciate, but take it further and notice what these things teach me about you. I don't know what to make of a God who can create both adorable baby buns and an old man's toenails, but you are awesome. I worship you for all you are. I love you. Amen.

No, No, No. Not Interested.

On Change

Do you ever look at a person, or a group of people, and find yourself mystified at their choices? Let's analyze the Pilgrims for a minute, a group that has always fascinated the fire out of me. To be honest, this fascination probably has a lot to do with originally learning about them in elementary school. If we were studying the Pilgrims it meant we weren't studying math or playing stupid games in gym class, so the Pilgrims were always the least of all my academic evils.

What fascinates me about these early settlers is that they left a place they knew for a place they didn't know at all. Although we've had almost four hundred years to digest their experience and identify where things went wrong, those poor adventurers had no clue of what they were about to experience. Experiences like rough seas, structural problems with the boat, surviving a horrible winter in the new land, sickness, and death, to mention a few.

Let's pause for a moment and consider one small fact about their voyage across the sea: the Mayflower had a hull approximately ninety feet long.[4] For reference, our family lives in a house that's roughly forty feet wide. If we double the width of this house and add a few feet, we're about the same size as the ship. If four people live comfortably in this forty-foot home now, then eight people could live here at the Mayflower size and squeeze a bit. Maybe even ten. Let's not forget the settlers had to bring all their provisions to live on board and in the new land, so a sizeable amount of available space would have been allocated to storage. This leaves precious little room for a hot tub and shuffleboard court.

According to my (admittedly dubious) calculations, the Mayflower should have fit sixteen to twenty passengers *at most*. But that poor, floating, wooden tub left England with 102 passengers and thirty crewmembers. That equals 132 individuals on a craft crossing the entire Atlantic Ocean.

I cannot imagine what possessed those people to board. I would have been a crazed woman on the dock, screeching in refusal. My skirt would have been swishing as I turned the opposite direction and headed for *any place* but that boat. It's insane. I wouldn't spend the weekend in a 106-foot ship with 131 other people. Two months at sea is completely unacceptable.

So the question is this: What motivated them to board? Why were they open to the idea at all? It had to be more than simply religious freedom or the need for more space, because I bet at least one place in continental Europe could have provided them those things, and with only a small hop across the English Channel. Their need for change must have been even bigger than a trip to France could provide.

They needed a total change, and they were willing to suffer whatever was required to get it.

I have no idea of what that's like, and I'm guessing you don't either. Mostly we resist change of any sort. If my husband's company transferred him to the branch in California I'd be having all kinds of fits, and we're talking about *California*. They have electricity, grocery stores, and flip-flops there. It's hardly different than here at all, and yet I'd come undone in spectacular and loud ways. Sobbing-in-the-kitchen-while-I-chop-lettuce kind of ways.

In her book, *Home Is Where My People Are*, author Sophie Hudson talks about this love of home and family, this love of what is familiar. She mentions driving through Birmingham one afternoon, where an SUV full of teenagers slowed down to yell, "HEYYYYY, MRS.

HUDSON!" at her as they hung out of the windows. She loved belonging in that place at that moment, but she'd also learned along the way
that belonging goes further than a familiar location. She writes:

> It's easy, I think, to go through life believing we can satisfy our
> longing for home with a three-bedroom, two-bath slice of the
> American dream that we mortgage at 4 percent interest and pay
> for over the course of thirty years. But it seems to me that, in
> our deepest places, what we're really looking for is to belong, to
> be seen, and to be known. And what we sometimes miss in all
> our searching for the perfect spot to set up camp, so to speak, is
> that wherever we are—whether it's short term or long term—
> we can count on the fact that God is at work in the journey.
>
> So here's what I know way down deep in my bones: at every
> stop in the road—no matter what the physical address happens
> to be—the Lord shows Himself to be so gracious. So loving.
> So intentional. So consistent. So kind. Even when our circum-
> stances aren't easy.[5]

I hear what she's saying. I want to believe God is intentional and
consistent and kind. But what if the change God asks me to make ends
up looking like 132 individuals on a wooden death trap, flopping wildly
over three thousand miles of water? That feels different than the benefi-
cent attributes of God Sophie refers to. It would feel more like random,
dice-throwing attributes, making sport of my future.

This goes far beyond simple matters of postal codes or sea voy-
ages, by the way. Sometimes we aren't asked to move to a new place,
but to live through something new—right where we're planted. We
might get to keep our grocery store and coffee shop, but we might be
headed to a totally new life in this place. It can be just as hard. Just as
heart-shattering.

I was reading in the book of Matthew recently, and the story of Jesus
calling the first disciples jumped out at me in a new way.

One day as Jesus was walking along the shore of the Sea of Galilee, he saw two brothers—Simon, also called Peter, and Andrew—throwing a net into the water, for they fished for a living. Jesus called out to them, "Come, follow me, and I will show you how to fish for people!" And they left their nets at once and followed him. A little farther up the shore he saw two other brothers, James and John, sitting in a boat with their father, Zebedee, repairing their nets. And he called them to come, too. They immediately followed him, leaving the boat and their father behind. (Matt. 4:18–22)

I suddenly had all kinds of questions when I read it this time, like *WHY*. Why did they do it? What made them put down the nets and pick up a whole new life? It could have been all manner of things. Perhaps they hated fish and had spent years planning a new career, but I doubt it. My understanding of ancient jobs is that a man pretty much did whatever his father had done before him, and a woman pretty much did what her mother had done. I don't think they were taking career assessment tests with the local community college advisors.

Here's the thing about Jesus—he brings change to every life he touches. It's a simple requirement of following him. Spiritually speaking, we're terribly, terribly grateful, because we remember what we were before we turned from ourselves and chose his way instead. We were lost. Lost, gross, and without hope. But choosing his direction, loveliness, and future always means we have to let go of ourselves and let him have his way with our lives. This is so, so hard. We want his way, without letting go of our way.

It's not possible. We have to choose.

And this is how the Pilgrims boarded a rickety, small, cramped boat and floated off to an unknown future. They traded what was familiar for what they were called to do. It's also how four fishermen set down nets and immediately picked up whatever Jesus was handing out.

It's how the abolitionists found the guts to fight for the end of slavery.

It's how participants in the Civil Rights movement had the courage to stand up and declare every color of skin had equal value. It's how the church will now find the Spirit-fueled energy to stay true to the Bible, even when modern culture insists we're irrelevant and intolerant.

Change is hard, but it brings what is necessary. Think of what our lives would be if all these people hadn't had the guts to change. Imagine if the fishermen had looked at Jesus and said, "No thanks. I'm super good at fishing." What if the abolitionists and those in the Civil Rights movement had chosen silence? It would have been a whole lot easier and more comfortable for them, that's for sure. But the results of their inaction would have been devastating for millions of people after them.

What happens if we choose silence and familiarity? I shudder to think of what will happen if we decide it's too hard to trust that Jesus will meet us in that new place.

To get us moving and trusting, I would like to offer two theories of why the disciples set down their nets and immediately followed the guy yelling at them from the shore. These are just my theories—I have no tidy passages from Scripture to back me up.

But I think that, first of all, the fishermen probably knew Jesus somehow. They were fishing in the Sea of Galilee, and we know that Jesus was from Nazareth in Galilee. The first chapter of John also tells us that John the Baptist had been declaring Jesus to be the Chosen One of God to his disciples. I think the chances are good that Jesus didn't pick his disciples by cold-calling random strangers out of their boats. I think they knew him, and knew there was something about him that bore trusting and deserved a chance.

But more importantly, I think God was working in their hearts long before Jesus started calling from the sand. It was part of what Yahweh had been doing for thousands of years, slowly establishing his perfect plan. John the Baptist felt it; the magi from the East had sought it. Herod had killed an entire region of boy babies because he feared it. God's plan was coming to fruition, one heart at a time.

God was at work, moving exactly the right people into place for exactly the right time. Peter, Andrew, James, and John were just four members of that movement. When Jesus called to them, their hearts were ready to respond.

> God was at work, moving exactly the right people into place for exactly the right time.

Could this be true for us today? If we truly know Jesus, would that make the stressful changes in our lives any easier? I think *yes*. To know Jesus is to recognize his provision and care even while we toss in the heaving sea. To truly know Jesus in the direst of situations is to trust and love him, knowing we can never see or understand the full scope of what is going on beyond our human understanding. We get to know Jesus this deeply by spending more time in his Word and with his church. More time than we spend with Netflix and HGTV, by the way.

I know, that was a low blow. I apologize a little bit for the sneak attack. But I'm not wrong. Sometimes we're stressed out with life's changes because we are too focused on the wrong things. If we're going to survive this new life, we have to be completely ready to dedicate time to learning more about the One we profess to follow. It takes time and prayer and a stillness of spirit so we can truly hear him and get to know him more.

And secondly, we need to understand that God is still bringing his plan together, one heart at a time. He places us into the right spot. He brings the right things. He calls to us at just the right times.

Believing this, I'd like to change my automatic response to change from "No, no, no, not interested," to "Okay, Lord." I'm not saying I'm interested in a trans-Atlantic journey in a rickety pile of lumber quite yet. I haven't had a lobotomy in the time between starting this chapter and now. But I'm willing to think about those four fishermen on their boats, and what motivated them to action.

"Come, follow me, and I will show you how to fish for people!" Jesus said. I wonder what he has planned for us.

Make It Personal

1. What stressful change are you agonizing over right now?
2. Look back over your life and think of three difficult changes you have had to make. How did things end up over the years? What would have happened if you hadn't made the changes?

Scripture Focus

"Then Jesus began to tell them that the Son of Man must suffer many terrible things and be rejected by the elders, the leading priests, and the teachers of religious law. He would be killed, but three days later he would rise from the dead. As he talked about this openly with his disciples, Peter took him aside and began to reprimand him for saying such things. Jesus turned around and looked at his disciples, then reprimanded Peter. 'Get away for me, Satan!' he said. 'You are seeing things merely from a human point of view, not from God's.' Then, calling the crowd to join his disciples, he said, 'If any of you wants to be my follower, you must give up your own way, take up your cross, and follow me. If you try to hang on to your life, you will lose it. But if you give up your life for my sake and for the sake of the Good News, you will save it'" (Mark 8:31–35).

A Prayer for Today

Heavenly Father, I'm not ready for the changes that are looming on the horizon. I like the familiar things. Anything could happen once I step out in faith, and what if it's awful? Please help me to stop hanging on to my life. Help me to remember the good news and my part in sharing it with the world. May I reflect Christ's example, because he knew the next change would bring temporary death, but eventually life. Help me to trust you like that. Amen.

At Least a Monarchy Doesn't Have a Two-Year Pre-Election Season

On Politics

Every morning at 5:45 my alarm clock snaps on to National Public Radio's litany of daily doom and gloom. Before my brain is even working, I'm bombarded with weather-related catastrophes, social upheaval, and—NPR's particular favorite—political turmoil. It's enough to make a person wonder if the world will end before lunch.

It turns out this fear is nothing new. Recently I was reading Henri Nouwen's book *¡Gracias!*, a compilation of his journal entries from time he spent in Latin America. Nouwen, a Catholic priest, felt like God might be calling him to serve in a completely new area of ministry. He visited several countries and wrote about his experience in vivid, moving detail. He fell in love with the people of Bolivia and Peru, and he quickly began to feel great concern over their unjust political systems. He wrote at length over their suffering and his fear for Latin America's future. He also wrote about his concerns for the United States, even wondering if the country could continue much longer. He feared complete political disintegration in the very near future.

His journal entries were written in 1981 and 1982. More than thirty-five years later, the United States is still trucking along. We're still fearing complete political disintegration, but hopefully in thirty years our political anxieties will sound just like Nouwen's concerns—wild speculations that never came true.

Not that long ago we endured a hotly contested firestorm of an election here in the United States. While I fully admit to enjoying every terrible joke and every *Saturday Night Live* skit, it was thoroughly unnerving to watch the election results roll in as we realized the next four years in America were about to look very different than most of us had anticipated. Some of us had deep-seated fears about who would lead our country, and they were all about to become reality.

Before your eyes glaze over at the thought of a political science lecture, let me assure you that my interest in politics is about zero. My *expertise* in politics registers considerably lower than that. My point here is one of stress reduction for you, my dear reader. Don't worry that I'm about to throw my political knowledge in your face, because I have precisely none of that. But I do know this: it may seem like our political systems are coming apart at the seams, but we were never meant to put our trust in political systems.

It's time for a reminder. It's time to identify our true citizenship. My friend Joseph lives in the United Kingdom, and although we live an ocean apart, we are both citizens of God's kingdom. Because of what Paul writes in his letter to the Ephesians, we know that we Gentiles used to be foreigners, excluded from citizenship among the people of Israel.

But now you have been united with Christ Jesus. Once you were far away from God, but now you have been brought near to him through the blood of Christ. For Christ himself has brought peace to us. He united Jews and Gentiles into one people when, in his own body on the cross, he broke down the wall of hostility that separated us. He did this by ending the system of law with its commandments and regulations. He made peace between Jews and Gentiles by creating in himself one new people from the two groups. Together as one body, Christ reconciled both groups to God by means of his death on the cross, and our hostility toward each other was put to death. . . . So now you Gentiles are no longer strangers and foreigners. You are citizens along with all of God's holy people. You are members of God's family. (Eph. 2:13–16, 19)

This must explain why I feel like a foreigner in my own country lately. I often have to choose between being a modern American and being a Christian, and I relentlessly desire to follow Christ. This means I'm often at odds with judicial decrees, modern laws, and every single magazine available in the checkout lane at the grocery store. I don't recognize any of it anymore.

May I be further, and more deeply, honest? Sometimes I don't even feel like I belong among proper church people any longer. I fear we've developed a Christian culture that's very full of churchy words and official churchy opinions and stances, but falls very, very short of our Messiah. You know, the One who sat with his friends and shared the truth and love of his Father over bread and wine. We have radio stations and T-shirts and weekend conferences where we reinforce our stances and opinions, and we mangle Scripture until it props up what we want to believe, but it doesn't really feel like being called into union with God's holy people by what Christ did for us on the cross.

It feels like a weird version of the world, not a heavenly kingdom. It feels like we've staked out our territory and are ready to defend our Christian culture to the death, but if we remember, we've already found our security. It doesn't come from anything here on earth. Our eternal security and citizenship rest in what Christ has done for us, not in how many religious memes we post on Facebook. We've lost our focus, and we desperately need to get it back. We serve a king who doesn't live in the White House or a castle in England. So let's live our lives and stop panicking over every report out of the Democratic National Convention, shall we?

We know the end. And it's nothing that radio announcers can report in their three minutes of doom each morning. This is all very, very temporary, but the eternal end has already been written for us.

> Our eternal security and citizenship rest in what Christ has done for us, not in how many religious memes we post on Facebook.

Not that we can sit around and ignore the world around us. We've been planted in this place and time, and we're still commissioned to bring the good news of Jesus Christ to the people around us. So, yes. We should absolutely be involved in politics, because politicians need to be surrounded by God's people. We need to be in the courts, the legislature, and elected positions just like we need to be on the football fields, in the hospitals, and in the schools. The more of us who are being salt and light to this generation, the better. Doesn't that take the pressure off a little? We're called to be salt and light, loving and truthful. I don't see that we're called to drag an entire nation's government back to the religious standards we find acceptable.

We're called to share the good news about Jesus. Paul himself advocated being a slave to all people to bring many to Christ. While with the Jews, he lived like a Jew. While with Gentiles, he lived like a Gentile. But no matter what his temporary cultural situation, in all things he obeyed the laws of Christ. "Yes, I try to find common ground with everyone, doing everything I can to save some. I do everything to spread the Good News and share in its blessings" (1 Cor. 9:22–23).

We need to be involved and we need to be prayerful. These poor fools who think they're running the government need every prayer we can send up for them. 1 Timothy 2:1–5 clarifies our position when Paul writes, "I urge you, first of all, to pray for all people. Ask God to help them; intercede on their behalf, and give thanks for them. Pray this way for kings and all who are in authority so that we can live peaceful and quiet lives marked by godliness and dignity. This is good and pleases

God our Savior, who wants everyone to be saved and to understand the truth. For, there is one God and one Mediator who can reconcile God and humanity—the man Christ Jesus."

The world is blind and scared and convinced more power is the solution to their problems, but we know better. Let's look at Isaiah 44 and 45, a powerful story of God's involvement in political leadership. In the passage, several times Cyrus is referenced in a way that seems like he's some sort of a puppet in God's hands. Which he most certainly was; God used him to do exactly what God wanted done. Cyrus the Great probably thought he was pretty big stuff, but God was on his almighty throne, leveling mountains and smashing down gates of iron for him.

How embarrassing for Cyrus. It makes me wonder how many things I've been proud of, when those successes have just been God in the background working out his plan. An honest evaluation would probably reveal that this applies to all the things I've ever done that have been worthwhile, just like Cyrus the Great.

Isaiah 45:13 says, "I will raise up Cyrus to fulfill my righteous purpose, and I will guide his actions. He will restore my city and free my captive people—without seeking a reward! I, the LORD of Heaven's Armies, have spoken!"

If God can use Cyrus like this, I don't see any reason to fear our modern political problems. Yes, things might get quite terrible here in the near future. Future generations might raise their eyebrows and say, "My, my. What a gigantic, horrid mess that must have been." NPR will never run out of impending catastrophes to report.

But I will not fear. I might shut down my Facebook account and refuse to check the news until Christmas of 2025, but I will not fear. And I hope you won't either.

Make It Personal

1. What do you think it means to be a citizen of God's kingdom? What does that look like while we're here on earth?

2. What do you think our eternal kingdom will be like? Imagine a

world where our King is the absolute authority. What do you hope we'll see, hear, and experience?

Scripture Focus

"I am the LORD; there is no other God. I have equipped you for battle, though you don't even know me, so all the world from east to west will know there is no other God. I am the LORD, and there is no other. I create the light and make the darkness. I send good times and bad times. I, the LORD, am the one who does these things" (Isa. 45:5–7).

A Prayer for Today

Dear King of heaven, I wish you would set up your eternal kingdom now. These people are crazy and I'm a little bit afraid of them. I certainly don't trust any of them. And while I don't understand all the undercurrents of politics, I know you do. I know you're not upset by what men are doing here on earth. Please remind me of your all-powerful, all-knowing love for us. Please be with our leaders. Go before them, direct them, and guide them. May your will be done, may your kingdom come. Amen.

Part 2

Other People and Their Chaos Stress Me Out

The Stress Others Cause Us

In case I haven't made it quite clear already, I need to state this fact: I am an introvert. I can work a to-do list from top to bottom for days at a time, but two hours with a lot of people wears me clean out.

I generally climb into the car after our small group meetings feeling like a small tornado has hit my brain. I love those families, but there are a million children and a million conversations and a million noodles on the floor after the kids are done eating. It's an explosion of children and pasta.

Honestly, we have only two children because this is the exact amount of chaos I can handle. I tip my hat to moms of three or more kids—you are stronger women than I am. Or, maybe you're the mom of one kid who equals three kids in terms of energy expended in any given day. I have a nephew like that. Jackson got a grappling hook for his eleventh birthday so he could climb trees (and buildings) more efficiently. His parents bought him one because he had been trying to make one out of odds and ends from the garage on his own. They figured a solidly manufactured hook was safer than something cobbled together with duct tape and lawn mower parts.

I am not making that up. Keeping up with that kid takes every ounce of strength the Lord has bestowed on his parents.

It's not just the kids who stress us out either. It's our siblings and parents and neighbors and coworkers. All human beings have the capacity to make our lives so much more difficult than they need to be, don't they? Sharing life and space with others is messy. Things get hard and arguing, whining, and noise ensue. We betray one another, gossip behind backs, and misunderstand others' intentions. We have drama queens, competitive frenemies, and that girl from middle school who still haunts our adult years.

Good gracious. It's a wonder any of us can stand to live in civilization. I'm beginning to think Pa Ingalls had the right idea as he headed out to the prairie, farther and farther away from neighbors. But at this point, the prairie already has a housing tract and a row of fast-food restaurants, so I'm not sure there's any place left to move.

Greenland, maybe? I hear that's still vastly underpopulated. But I also hear it's a giant rock coated in ice, and the July temperatures barely crack fifty-five degrees Fahrenheit, so I guess I'll take my chances with my crazy people.

If you decide to move to Greenland you probably won't need this next section of the book. Email me and let me know how the transition is going, and also let me know if you've found any good recipes for seal.

For the rest of us who are doomed to civilization and daily doses of chaos from our loved ones, let's see if God's way of working with us, his stubborn and frustrating children, has any insights for us. It has to be a better option than a move to an icy rock.

Just Be Quiet and Agree with Me

On Arguing and Conflict

I HAVE A friend who never backs down from a fight. He doesn't go looking for trouble specifically, so we never have to bail him out of jail late at night or let him hide in our basement from angry mobs. But if there's ever a reason to rumble, my friend is stepping up to the line. He thinks it's fun. He's quick-witted, opinionated, and smart as a whip. He also has biceps the size of my head, so in any kind of fight—physical or mental—he's able to take his opponent down.

I like to hide behind him occasionally when things get ferocious. I have spent four decades learning how to avoid conflict at all costs, so it's nice to have someone like him around when things get sticky. It's also a little unnerving, because occasionally I can see the spot where we can diffuse the situation but he's already charging in, flexing his muscles and sharpening his tongue. Sometimes I need to dart in front of him, saving him from himself. We make a pretty good team.

As much as I'd like to pretend utopia is possible (and trust me, I'd really, *really* like this to be the case), where everyone walks around in a fog of cooperation and joyful negotiation, that's not the world we actually live in. We get a lot more arguing and conflict here. I comfort myself with the knowledge that even Jesus himself, our precious Lord and Savior, walked the earth with twelve goobers who couldn't keep themselves from arguing as he walked right next to them.

If Jesus had to deal with goobers, then so will we. It's a fact of life. I think we imagine Jesus as a robed man with a hipster beard, wandering meekly through the crowds while he healed and taught. A gentle Jesus, if you will. While that was certainly part of his ministry, we tend to forget the Jesus who stood before the crowds and announced that he came to bring a sword, not peace to the world. In Matthew 10:34–36, he told listeners that he had come to set sons against their fathers, daughters against mothers, and in-laws against themselves. Hardly the sweet, gentle man in a robe we remember from our Sunday school lessons, right?

When Jesus said this, he was sending his disciples out to minister in the surrounding towns. But he sent them out with a warning—not everyone was going to welcome their message. They were headed into conflict, and Jesus was ready for it. But Jesus was ready for the right kind of conflict—the kind of conflict that comes when generations of hard-headedness bumps into the truth of the coming kingdom of God.

We mere humans tend to fight over things like how hot the sanctuary is and whether the choir needs to wear robes and what translation of the Bible is used in the sermon. We have church splits over the kind of music we play and whether a fog machine is allowed or not.

Of course, arguments aren't limited to the church family. Our nuclear and extended families fight over things like inheritances and debt and whether we feel like our personal destinies and happiness are being nourished.

We battle our neighbors over fence lines and annoying pets and have community warfare over zoning ordinances and noise pollution from the truck stop.

Jesus didn't back down from righteous conflict. We rarely get anywhere near righteous conflict because we're too busy fighting over stupid stuff. As long as we're alive, we're going to run into conflict of some sort. But what if we could skip over the inconsequential and save our energy for what matters? And, when we have to rumble over the really important stuff, what if we could do it the right way? Wouldn't that reduce our stress by a lot? I think it would. While I fully realize we will never be like Jesus, as he was perfect and we are quite less than that, I think we can take a few cues from his approach to trouble. He was firmly focused on the right things, all the time. He wanted to glorify his Father in all things, and he wanted to love others. Right away, I see our problem. Fights over choir robes don't even register on the scale if our goal is to glorify our heavenly Father.

> Jesus didn't back down from righteous conflict. We rarely get anywhere near righteous conflict because we're too busy fighting over stupid stuff.

I've always found it interesting that Jesus argued with the Pharisees all the time. Remember the story from Matthew 12, when the disciples ate some grain as they walked through the fields on the Sabbath? The Pharisees were on Jesus in a flash, demanding to know how his followers dared to break a commandment right in front of him. But Jesus, ever focused on honoring God and loving others, gave them a little lecture and ended it with, "I want you to show mercy, not offer sacrifices" (Matt. 12:7).

Ouch. He quoted Scripture right back at them because he knew it better than they did, because he wrote it. It was his book. And he knew it from the heart, not from the rulebooks that allowed personal striving to come before a heart that seeks and honors God.

The Pharisees never did get over themselves. They were right there at the very end, manipulating the government into crucifying Jesus and then trying to cover up the nasty details. I know we want better than that in our own lives. We don't want to be completely focused on our own understanding, comfort, and prestige like those religious leaders. I know we want to choose differently and filter our responses to conflict like Jesus did.

I sit here typing these words very piously, but here's what's actually going to happen. The next time someone antagonizes me, I'm going to serenely remind myself to honor God and honor this child of God right in front of me.

This moment will last for a fraction of a second.

Then my human impulses will rage to the surface, and I will cry from my soul, "But I must vanquish this foe! She stands between me and my personal happiness!" And my ears will do that thing where it feels like the waves of the ocean are suddenly in my skull.

This is where I will have two choices. I can choose God's way and get over myself, or I can choose that pesky personal happiness that trips me up every time. I am now forty years old, so I've lived with the pain of choosing myself for quite a long time. The lessons feel a lot like a child learning from touching a hot stove, and I'm starting to learn from the pain.

If my spiritual life is anywhere near what it should be, and if I've learned anything at all, I'll recognize the Holy Spirit when he steps in and reminds me that life in Christ is not about fighting for my own personal happiness or opinion. That just causes stress and furthers the divide. Instead, I can choose the way of Christ and reduce my own angst at the same time. Sure, for the moment it involves sacrificing my personal happiness, but you know what? I never miss it when things settle out. I have never regretted submitting to the Holy Spirit when he reminds me to choose love and honor. Never once. There is a higher option than personal happiness. There's something more dear than winning a round. There is peace that passes understanding, and we never find it by beating other people into the dust.

I'm hoping that as I work through inconsequential conflict the right way, I'll also get better at handling discord over important matters. It's apparent to all of us in the modern church that our culture is quickly turning against us. We're about to enter a time of deepening conflict over things that really matter, and I don't think it's going to be a minor skirmish. The church has been mightily persecuted before, and we might be heading into another round. I believe that Jesus's example holds true, no matter the situation.

Even as our culture turns against us, can we love and honor our non-Christian neighbors with the yappy dog and the tree that dumps walnuts on our property? I want us to walk through our communities knowing we've done our best to love the kids in the schools, the cashiers at the store, and the waitress at our table. It's my prayer that when media portrays Christians as hateful, intolerant jerks, our neighbors realize those people on the news bear no resemblance to the loving Christians who live next door or eat scrambled eggs at the diner on Thursday mornings. The apostle Peter said it this way: "Be careful to live properly among your unbelieving neighbors. Then even if they accuse you of doing wrong, they will see your honorable behavior, and they will give honor to God when he judges the world" (1 Peter 2:12).

When the day inevitably comes that we must stand for Christ in a world that has turned against him, may we still choose to honor God and love others. I have a feeling at this point we won't be fighting over fog machines or choir robes anymore, because our situation will have focused our attention like a laser beam on the right things. Stupid arguments will be a thing of the past.

But who really knows? The disciples found time to get sidetracked and have petty little fights as they matched Jesus step for step. Maybe our tendency to fight over the small things is inevitable. We could be doomed until the kingdom really does come and saves us from ourselves.

I hope not. I think we'll be doing the world and ourselves a favor when we choose to stop picking fights and getting worked up over the inconsequential. Honor God; honor others. Even if it means a fog machine is coughing out vapor during the worship service.

Make It Personal

1. Are you a fighter or a lover? How does that affect your life when you come up against real or petty conflict?

2. How important is your personal happiness? Does it interfere with your spiritual life or other relationships? How?

Scripture Focus

"Bless those who persecute you. Don't curse them; pray that God will bless them. Be happy with those who are happy, and weep with those who weep. Live in harmony with each other. Don't be too proud to enjoy the company of ordinary people. And don't think you know it all! Never pay back evil with more evil. Do things in such a way that everyone can see you are honorable. Do all that you can to live in peace with everyone. Dear friends, never take revenge. Leave that to the righteous anger of God" (Rom. 12:14–19).

For further study, read Matthew 10:32–42.

A Prayer for Today

Heavenly Father, I need the Holy Spirit's intervention here so badly. Conflict is so hard to handle well, especially in the heat of the moment. May I be brave when it matters, but may I also be willing to let go of things that are inconsequential. Help me to get over myself. Help me to look beyond my personal happiness. Please never leave my side when your name is called into question. Give me your words and strength when righteous conflict is unavoidable. Amen.

My Head Will Explode If I Hear One More Noise from You

On Chaos and Noise

ONCE UPON A time, there was a little boy who always hated his dinner. It made him cry. The noodles made him sad, the sauces made him weep, and any sort of chicken that looked like it had actually been a part of a living creature gave him fits. Every night he would come to the kitchen when summoned, take one good look at the night's offering, and then begin to wail and whimper at what he was about to endure.

Now, his mother knew she was no master chef. But no one had ever died from her food, so eventually she got sick of this nonsense. "You will eat this food and be happy about it!" she commanded. This solved nothing.

One day the little boy found a way to sidestep this nightly debacle. He would come to the kitchen, peer closely at dinner, then abruptly turn around and head for the bathroom. He'd pretend to poop for at least ten minutes, and then he would come out and quietly make himself a cheese sandwich.

His mother would gently rest her forehead on the table and silently evaluate her entire life and every decision she had ever made. She would wonder aloud if their family could live off cheeseburgers until they all died, as that appeared to be the only meal the entire family enjoyed.

The little boy didn't notice because his cheese sandwich was very yummy.

The end.

It is exactly this kind of completely fictional-ish story that is going to be the death of me. I shall surely perish from the whining and chaos and noise that emerge from the human beings who share my space with me.

I just want everyone to be happy.

And quiet. If they can't be happy, at least they can be quiet.

Amen.

You may have similar experiences, even if you're not a mother. Maybe you have really noisy neighbors. Perhaps you work in a zoo and the monkeys get out of control after breakfast. Schoolteacher? Prison guard? Congressperson? We all have our noise and chaos, and we all have the need to retreat far, far away from the commotion. To catch our breath and rest for a few moments.

Do you know who else had to take a moment to himself? Our dear Lord and Savior, Jesus Christ. Yes, Jesus, that perfect example of God's love in human form, had to take a moment to get away. Right there in the first chapter of Mark, Jesus got up early and snuck out. Just before that he'd been finding disciples, casting out evil spirits, and healing strangers and beloved friends alike.

Jesus was tired. The crowds were relentless. The needs ran deep. He was starting to develop a reputation, and the people were starting to ask a lot of questions. Even the demons were getting agitated. Jesus needed a moment to pray, so he headed out on his own before anyone else was awake. He needed to refuel.

Jesus could have done a lot of things, but he chose to pray. It was that person-to-person connection with the Father he needed more than anything else. I don't know about you, but my refueling moments tend to look like ten minutes on Facebook (which turns into an hour), two shows on Netflix about building tiny houses, and analyzing floor plans of beach cabins. The emotional equivalent of junk food, in other words. I think I could do better.

I think all of us can attest to the fact that if we feed our physical bodies with healthy, nourishing food, we feel great. We feel light as air, like one of those ladies in an ad for multivitamins. If we eat a pound of bacon and a bag of Cheetos, and then have an ice cream sundae, we feel like death. I think too many of us are refueling our spirits just like that, and we wonder why our souls are lardy, slow, cranky, and a little bit constipated.

What if we spent our precious few quiet moments on things that refueled our spirits well? I'm not saying all our free time needs to be spent in prayer, but that's a good place to start for a portion of the time. We could read the Bible or other books from thoughtful Christian authors. How about a nap? (Jesus napped, thank you very much.) We could take a walk or get some other form of exercise. Running, maybe? I hear people run for fun. We could meet a friend for coffee or *take a nap*.

Wait, did I mention that already? Can we take a moment to talk about naps? They're glorious. I love them so much. Today I didn't get a nap, and I can feel myself crashing already. I'm never going to make it through the evening. I used to feel guilty about my napping habit, until I learned a lot of really productive people nap almost every day. I give you permission right this minute—if you need a nap, take a nap. Your body, mind, spirit, and family will thank you.

> I used to feel guilty about my napping habit, until I learned a lot of really productive people nap almost every day.

I know it might feel like the chaos will grow even worse if you fall asleep on the job, which might be true, honestly. You might wake up and find the children have shaved the cat or maybe even each other. But the kids will probably get into shenanigans no matter what you do, right? You can turn your back for thirty tiny seconds and they'll destroy something. You might as well be well rested as you scream.

We serve a God who built the Sabbath rest into the very beginning of his creation. He made it all, and then he rested. He teaches us to do the same, and not because he's an angry old man who wants everyone to shush up for an entire day each week. It's because he loves us and knows us so deeply that he understands our need for quiet, for silence, for a break from the madness. The Sabbath teaches us how to stop our daily grind and to set aside specific time to seek God.

I'm not going to get into a diatribe about legalistic rules about the Sabbath. We have friends who joyfully set aside the entire day—no shopping, no eating out, no buying gas. Just rest. We have other friends who go to church and then go right into work. Eric and I fit somewhere in the middle, where we go to church, but sometimes Eric has to work a four-hour shift before the service. It's rare; we don't beat ourselves up when it happens. The point is that we rest, we refocus, and we reorder our world in a regular pattern each week. We line ourselves back up with God's best as much as possible. Sometimes we goof it up and exhaust ourselves even when we're not working, so the balance can be hard to find. We haven't perfected it yet.

But we aren't giving up on our search for rest, even if we do occasionally come home from a "relaxing" day all pooped out and cranky and sunburned. That's the thing about God; he built this rest into every week. We get to try again in just a few days. They might be a long, draining six days, but we'll get through them and try again.

I'm sure there will still be days when I forget and turn to my Instagram feed instead of prayer. I know I'll choose the spiritual equivalent of Cheetos over the solid, chewy, life-giving Word of God. But little by little, I'm trying to open my eyes and realize what my soul and body need, and then respond well.

And as always, I'll be napping on the couch most days from two thirty to three, hoping it will give me the strength to get through tonight's inevitable scene at the dinner table. When I've had some rest, I can conquer any chaos and I can make it through any amount of noise. For a little while, at least.

Make It Personal

1. Where do you go when you're tired and need a moment to yourself? What can you do to institute ways to gain refreshment?

2. Think of a person who seems calm, rested, and unperturbed amid chaos. Why do you think that is? What can you learn from her example?

Scripture Focus

"That evening after sunset, many sick and demon-possessed people were brought to Jesus. The whole town gathered at the door to watch. So Jesus healed many people who were sick with various diseases, and he cast out many demons. . . . Before daybreak the next morning, Jesus got up and went out to an isolated place to pray" (Mark 1:32–35).

A Prayer for Today

Heavenly Father, my soul is craving quiet and rest. I'm overwhelmed with the needs and the noise. My brain feels like I'm living in the monkey house at the zoo, and I'm headed for a meltdown soon. I can't keep everyone happy and keep my sanity at the same time. Please help me to turn to you to refuel my spirit. May you give me peace, grace, and rest. Amen.

I Never Said That

On Misunderstandings

ONE OF MY kids, the girl one, is deaf as a post. She had a doctor's appointment yesterday and the man looked into her ear holes without concern, so I'm assuming all the equipment is functional in there. But something is being lost in translation.

"Audrey, have you seen my gray socks?" prompts a puzzled look from her.

"What did you say about Grace's box?"

"GRAY. Gray. Soooooccccckkkksssss," I repeat slowly, so her non-functioning ear holes can catch up.

"Why would I have your socks? They don't go with anything I wear."

I think the better question would be, why do I try to talk to this girl? She can't hear anything. You know what works really well for us? Texting. The child can see just fine. There's nothing wrong with her brain's ability to understand information when it comes in optically, so that's going to be our default communication method until my fingers become too arthritic to text. Then I guess we'll just go back to shouting slowly at each other, enunciating all the challenging sounds. I'm sure it will be fine. Not annoying at all.

Actually, I do think Audrey's ears are working okay, but I also think she's thirteen and a completely distracted human being. Her brain is whirring along at top speed, constantly analyzing her friends' social media posts, the latest YouTube video she watched with her brother, and characters from a novel. Occasionally some information about schoolwork or the Bible pops in and out of that chaos, but mostly she's thinking about friends, both real and virtual.

Welcome to thirteen-year-olds, I guess. Not that we get much better at this as we age. A few weeks ago, we had a minor but complicated issue at the church where I work, so I spent some time carefully crafting my email to the pastors and elders. I reread it three times and tweaked it until I had succinctly communicated everything essential. It was a masterpiece. Well, until one of the pastors read it and came away with the absolute opposite understanding of what I'd meant. I almost smashed my head on my desk with the agony of failing in the communication department.

That's the only skill I bring to my job! I can't actually type very quickly or take minutes or write shorthand. I can vaguely file things away (pray for the secretaries who come after me), and I answer the phone when I feel like it. If I'm not actually helping the congregation to communicate, then essentially I am being paid to keep the airspace in my little office moving. The church is not getting their money's worth, in other words.

Maybe it's because I'm a writer and communicating is my thing, but I bet you also have a deep need to be understood. And I think most of us dearly want to understand others. We desire to deeply and truly know the people around us, but it's all so complicated. We speak, and no one *gets it*. Maybe our words get muddled or twisted. Sometimes I think I've said all the words, when really my loved ones have no idea what I mean because I've been thinking my thoughts, not verbalizing them. Layers and layers of miscommunication lead to hard feelings, stress, and tension.

Have you seen that cartoon with the husband and wife lying in bed? She's on her side, quietly going insane while she wonders what he's thinking. She wonders why he's silent. She assumes he's tense, thinking about how terrible their marriage is. She begins to worry he doesn't love her anymore and their marriage is over. She's going to be abandoned by the weekend.

He's over on his side, thinking about why the transmission in the car is making that weird noise.

Yes, exactly this.

Ladies, sometimes we're making ourselves crazy for no good reason. We buy our ticket to Crazytown and take the Crazy Bus straight there, even though we're the only person on the sidewalks. But other times the problems are real, and we really are having trouble communicating. I don't know that there's much we can do about this, honestly. As humans we're distracted, overwhelmed, and completely focused on our own thing. We find ourselves in the car with the kids yelling, the phone beeping, and the husband trying to talk to us. Which thing are we supposed to pay attention to? All of it at once? It's impossible.

It's my new lifelong mission to learn to listen. I will need to practice this until I am dead, and I know I'll never really perfect it. But that's where I'm starting. I was reading the Bible when I noticed how many times Jesus begged his followers to listen, truly listen, to his words. So much important stuff begins with that one thing—silencing our own thoughts to focus on what is being presented to our ear holes. We need to pay attention with our hearing apparatuses and our hearts, pushing our own opinions away for the moment.

It's so hard, but it's so important. And we can spend our lives perfecting the art of listening, but that doesn't mean the people around us will. They'll still be distracted and deafened by their own life. Their opinions will muddle anything we're trying to communicate. The only thing we can do is try again. Every time there's a misunderstanding, it's up to someone (probably us) to try one more time. In Ephesians 4:1–6, Paul calls the church to unity and lives worthy of the calling we have received. When he said to always be humble and gentle, to be patient, and to make allowances for each other because of our love, I think he was talking about these exact misunderstandings.

Honestly, I'm not that excited about this idea. Half the time I talk to my kids and the conversation goes nowhere, so I simply turn around and say, "I'm not talking to you anymore." Then we drop the conversation. Talking is hard. It's aggravating. And some of us have been (barely) communicating with the same poor ragged bunch of fools for decades! How many times do we have to try again?

Paul doesn't give an exact number, but he does go on to say this later in Ephesians 4: "And do not bring sorrow to God's Holy Spirit by the way you live. Remember, he has identified you as his own, guaranteeing that you will be saved on the day of redemption. Get rid of all bitterness, rage, anger, harsh words, and slander, as well as all types of evil behavior. Instead, be kind to each other, tenderhearted, forgiving one another, just as God through Christ has forgiven you" (vv. 30–32).

I would have dearly appreciated if our friend, the apostle Paul, could have set the standard a wee bit lower, because this is a lot to digest. I know how much Christ has forgiven in my own life, but it's still really difficult to apply that same sort of forgiveness to the issues I face with others. Do I have to be tenderhearted like Jesus? Do I have to be kind like Jesus?

> If my heart is motivated by love for everyone in my path, I fare a far better chance of understanding and being understood.

I think I do. And as I think it through, all of this comes down to one thought. It's all about my motivations. What motivates me as I speak and listen to others? No matter how hard I try to listen or be like Jesus, I'm just one sassy redhead who can't get it together. I'm going to goof this up. But if my heart is motivated by love for everyone in my path, I fare a far better chance of understanding and being understood.

Does Christ's love for me motivate me to love others? Does his compassion motivate me to listen with grace and intensity? Does his sacrifice motivate me to get over myself and try again?

If yes, then when I do mess up and misunderstand, things are still fixable. Love covers a multitude of sins and mistakes. If my people know I love them and I'm genuinely trying, then they're going to be far more willing to show me the grace I need as I struggle to do my best for them.

But if they suspect I'm secretly motivated by selfishness and greed, things aren't going to end well. My motivations and heart toward them are going to make the difference in our relationship. Misunderstandings only get worse when we aren't listening and speaking with love. We can't avoid communication problems, but we can minimize the effects.

Elizabeth Gilbert once wrote a little book called *Eat, Pray, Love*. The book became a best seller and eventually a movie, detailing her account of progressing from an anxious woman struggling through a nasty divorce to finding peace and joy in her travels around the world. While her story is definitely not the makings of an evangelical turn-to-Jesus memoir, she does chronicle the events in a deeply personal, authentic way. It is her story.

One day a reader approached Gilbert to express her gratitude for *Eat, Pray, Love*. Specifically, the fan wanted Gilbert to know a certain part of the book had changed her life. She said that because the author had left her abusive husband, this had given the reader the strength to leave her own abusive marriage. Gilbert was flabbergasted, because while her first marriage was terrible, it certainly wasn't *abusive*. She'd not written any such thing into the book. It had never happened! The reader had taken her own issues and inserted them into Gilbert's story.[6]

Isn't that just the way it goes? Our lives are always shouting in our own ears, hindering our ability to sort out what others are saying. And they're having the same problem over there in their own heads. It's madness, I tell you. I can't promise we'll be able to solve it, but we can try to listen out of love, and do it over and over again. Maybe one day we'll actually be able to understand one another.

Make It Personal

1. What's harder for you—listening well or communicating your thoughts well? Why?

2. What are your deepest, heartfelt motives toward others? Are any misunderstandings fixable with a commitment to genuinely care for them? How, specifically, can you put that into action?

Scripture Focus

"A tree is identified by its fruit. If a tree is good, its fruit will be good. If a tree is bad, its fruit will be bad. You brood of snakes! How could evil men like you speak what is good and right? For whatever is in your heart determines what you say. A good person produces good things from the treasury of a good heart, and an evil person produces evil things from the treasury of an evil heart. And I tell you this, you must give an account on judgment day for every idle word you speak. The words you say will either acquit you or condemn you" (Matt. 12:33–37).

For further study, read Ephesians 4:1–6.

A Prayer for Today

Heavenly Father, help me to listen. Help me to love. May my motivations be pure, seeking to benefit the ones who speak to me. Motivate me to be more like Jesus, genuinely caring for others. Please help me to try again when we experience misunderstandings. Amen.

Could You Just Wake Up and Be Normal for a Change?

On Drama

Please close your eyes and take a little trip with me, back to the golden days of my childhood. My grandmother shared a little ranch house with her sister in a suburb of Detroit. Like most of their neighbors they were solidly middle class, Catholic, and Polish. They smoked cigarettes by the pack and started cocktail hour at 4 p.m. every day. Mass on Sundays was celebrated with a stop at the local grocery store for a box of doughnuts, and they stocked up on 7-Up with every shopping trip. They had a little poodle named MeMo who yapped a lot and wasn't super excited about small children.

Because it was the mid eighties, the seventies still had a firm grip on the decorating situation in their house. The carpet was a golden-orange shag. The bathroom fixtures, walls, and floor were avocado green, and the end of the hallway had a marbled floor-to-ceiling mirror. Please do not forget the aforementioned cigarette smoking, which added the final layer of atmosphere and charm.

This may be why I don't get upset when someone smokes near me. I inhale deeply and think, "I *miss* you, Grandma. You and that terrible pattern on the couch."

My great-aunt spent a lot of time on that floral couch. She grew increasingly ill as she aged, so she spent most of her time resting. The television kept her company—news anchors and game show hosts in the morning, soap opera divas all afternoon. *Oh, the glory.* We'd join her in that haven of questionable decorating choices, smoke hanging around our heads, sipping small cups of 7-Up that Grandma would bring us.

My mother was far too busy and far too practical to watch soap operas at home. Not to mention that she found 90 percent of the content morally offensive, and she certainly didn't want to pass that trash on to her kids. But there wasn't much she could do about it when we were at someone else's house. Mom tried to get us busy with other things, but sometimes she just gave up and let us watch.

Hey, a woman gets tired. She probably hoped that fifty-two hours of Sunday school each year would overcome a few hours of trashy TV next to an elderly aunt. She was (mostly) right and we (mostly) turned out okay.

I loved the hushed, intense conversations on my great-aunt's soaps. I loved not knowing who would end up dead—or back alive—by the end of the show. I was fascinated with secret twin brothers and evil bosses. The clothes were so fancy and the fights were so shocking. It was all just so dramatic and fun.

I had no idea people actually lived like this. I thought it was all just made up for television and bored old ladies. It certainly didn't resemble anything I knew from my daily existence.

Now I'm an adult and realize some people really do aspire to this level of drama on a daily basis. They're basically 1980s soap queens, dressed in yoga pants instead of silk pantsuits, and Ugg boots instead of stilettos. Some of our local drama queens (or kings) are schlepping their kids around to preschool, or they're church members who run the choir. Quiet, mild-mannered citizens by day, but dramatic, conflict-seeking, exasperating morons by night. They can only hide for so long before their true personalities shine through.

Social media outs them. Their cell phone conversations betray them.

The wild-eyed, frantic looks of the other parents at soccer practice send clear warning signs: This person is not stable. Steer clear! Steer clear!

Hold up. Let's take a little break right here to discuss social media, shall we? I need to get something off my chest. Everyone gets exasperated every once in a while and vents into their cell phone. You can't help what others overhear when they eavesdrop. And everyone has a bad day here and there and acts like a fool. It happens. We're never going to be perfect. We frighten the people around us sometimes and that's just the way it is.

But social media is a chance to think clearly and carefully before posting any thought, political view, or photo. Did you catch that? It's a chance to think clearly before posting. To post on Facebook you have to be near a device. You have to pull up the app. You have to type in something or find the photo. And then you have to hit "post." That's four chances to make a good decision!

> Social media is a chance to think clearly and carefully before posting any thought, political view, or photo. Did you catch that?

And yet. How do we explain the negativity and drama that fill our social media feeds? How does anyone feel like it's okay to spew venom and craziness? I feel like I have a new way to read the pulse of my friends' mental stability, don't you? And I'm afraid. I am so, so afraid. A few of them are one step away from waking up from a yearlong coma to find her evil, secret twin sister is now married to her husband.

Thank goodness for the ability to shut devices down. It's like a mute button for the crazy. Quite helpful.

Some of us, though, aren't so lucky as to only be connected to drama queens through the internet. Some of us live next door to the problem, reside in the same house as the problem, or are legally or genetically linked to the problem. There's no escape. They're always staring at you over the turkey dinner during the holidays, and you're trapped.

Just reading that sentence probably has a few of you reaching for the laptop. You're about to start researching flights to the Bahamas for Christmas this year, aren't you? You're thinking that a beach resort with helpful maids who bring you fresh towels sounds way better than another meal listening to Aunt Edna complain about her children, or your cousin Matilda explain why she got fired three times this year without being at fault.

Of course, it's never their fault. Drama queens never realize when they cause their own problems.

Everyone else sees it, and we're tired of getting dragged into it. Short of leaving town for the holidays, is there anything we can do? How do we draw healthy, loving, and godly boundaries? Do we even know what those boundaries look like?

I think those boundaries start with what Paul writes in Philippians 4:8–9: "And now, dear brothers and sisters, one final thing. Fix your thoughts on what is true, and honorable, and right, and pure, and lovely, and admirable. Think about things that are excellent and worthy of praise. Keep putting into practice all you learned and received from me—everything you heard from me and saw me doing. Then the God of peace will be with you."

I don't know about you, but this is the kind of life I want to live. I want my heart and thoughts to be fixed on what is good and admirable, and then I want my words, actions, and social media posts to follow. Fine. Good. But we're not talking about me here. We're talking about those lunatics who make us crazy with their drama. What do we do when another person's negative attitude smashes into our own little happy self?

We begin with prayer. We pray that our hearts will indeed be focused on what Jesus taught us to do, which is to love God and to love others, and to seek humility and service and kindness. If we don't have the Holy Spirit's help to get our hearts in the right place, we're going to get dragged into the quagmire of negativity. We'll either cave and join the gossip, or we'll overreact and spend the rest of the day feeling like our nerves were popped in the microwave.

Once we've asked the Holy Spirit for help with our own attitude, we can pray for our friend. It's possible she doesn't realize she's causing so much fuss. She might have been raised in a home where there really were evil twin sisters and screaming fights in the funeral parlor. This might be normal life for her. We can pray that the Holy Spirit helps her to realize it's possible to set her mind on what is pure and lovely and honorable.

We can also pray that we model Christ's example to her. We can ask for help with wise responses and healthy, God-honoring conversations. This relationship might be turned around with our faithful response to what we learn in the Bible. We need to live out what we read in there, and when we do, lives are changed. The Holy Spirit can work through us to do amazing things!

But this kind of situation doesn't always have a happy ending. Sometimes there's no change. We might need to pray for the wisdom to step back from the conversation or relationship. My friend Peter made a comment to me the other day that really woke me up. He said (very kindly), "But you always engage with them." He was referring to my tendency to interact extensively with people—even if they've crossed the line of negativity or drama. He's right. I'll carry on a conversation for far too long because I don't want to hurt someone's feelings or make them feel unloved. But Peter noticed what I had not seen: sometimes a person needs to be left without a conversational partner so they can run out of negative fuel. If I engage, I'm only encouraging them.

It's a fine line we need to draw. Of course we don't want to abandon friends or family who are having a rough time. Heaven knows I've spent enough years (*years*, I tell you) inflicting myself on my friends and family when I hit a tough spot. They never left me. But they never encouraged me to wallow in my negativity either. I was fortunate enough that they modeled Christ-like behavior and encouraged me to focus on what was true, honorable, right, pure, lovely, and admirable. The God of peace is now with me, and I am forever grateful.

I pray the same for your situation, your drama queen, and your heart.

Make It Personal

1. Do you have some friends on social media who need to be hidden from your feed? Go and do that now, especially if you can do it without hurting their feelings. Trust me, you'll feel so much better.
2. Scroll through your recent social media posts, or think through recent conversations you've had. Where do you need to tone down the drama or the negativity?

Scripture Focus

"And now, dear brothers and sisters, one final thing. Fix your thoughts on what is true, and honorable, and right, and pure, and lovely, and admirable. Think about things that are excellent and worthy of praise. Keep putting into practice all you learned and received from me— everything you heard from me and saw me doing. Then the God of peace will be with you" (Phil. 4:8–9).

A Prayer for Today

Heavenly Father, I need so much wisdom. I don't want to be dragged into negativity and drama, because I know it doesn't please you. I certainly don't want to be the cause of negativity or drama either, and forgive me for where I have failed. Please give me your wisdom to recognize it and respond in a way that pleases you. May I love my friends and family without encouraging them to be negative. Amen.

Please Note How Amazing I Am

On Competition

EVERY ONCE IN a while, you can find my mother-in-law plopped down on her living room carpet playing a game with the family. She does this not because she enjoys games but because she loves her family. I wait for the inevitable moment when she stops chatting with whoever is nearby, clues back into the game, and demands to know, "Did I win?"

It makes us laugh every time.

She *never* wins. Usually the kids have skipped her and played on while Grandma talks to Aunt Wilma. She's not into rules or details, and I'm not sure she's ever had a competitive moment in her life. I think she moves her game piece backward when no one is looking so she can lose more quickly. Anything to end the game faster. No one's ever accused Grandma of being cutthroat.

Always wary of competitive people, I find this woman to be endearing beyond words. How can you not love a mother-in-law who tries to *lose*? There's no pressure with her—not in housekeeping, parenting, or even baking. She never tries to keep up with the other grannies, never pushes us to make her look good, never cares about appearances. She's wonderful, I tell you. But she's also the minority. Most people care a lot about those things, and turn their lives into little competitions to see who can win at their weird little games.

When I asked all my Facebook friends about what stressed them out, someone mentioned competition. But I don't think we're talking about soccer or Monopoly or a pie-baking competition here. If that sort of battle is your thing, then go with God, my sister. Out-run, out-strategize, and out-bake all your opponents. Smoke 'em. I think my friend was referring not to healthy competition but to what we all face every day in life. It rears its ugly head in all sorts of ways, from attempting to keep up with the Joneses, to posting only the best photos on social media, to silently keeping score with friends in general conversation.

For example, the Shiny Item Collection Game. Object of game: gather as many things as possible before you die. Items might actually be shiny, or just attractive in some manner so that others notice. See also: newest minivan, trendiest jeans, or most expensive granite countertops. Items should be expensive, others should be able to sense that immediately, and the item should be on display at all times.

Or, how about this one—the Social Media Popularity Game. Played among normal folks, the rules are simple but relentless—collect as many likes and friends as possible. Document every moment of life as if it's post-worthy. Be sure to only show the happy, clean, successful moments. The expert level (for writers and other professionals): Quickly and decisively gather a list of other professionals who do what you do. Rank them obsessively, noting not the message of any given post, but how many of their followers like or comment. Keep tabs on how many total followers they have across social media platforms. Keep score, making sure that "people" are actually turned to "numbers."

Let's not forget the Sneaky Ninja Mom Battle; the object of the game is to prove to everyone that your family is the best—but sneakily. Bonus points are awarded for false modesty and subtlety. Your children are the most precious. Your teens are the best students. Your marriage is the most romantic. You simply need to prove this to us with every post. Advanced levels include prestigious schools and careers. The ultimate glory should be recorded on social media if you can get your children to graduate from fancy schools and then take a vacation from their fabulous jobs so the whole family can celebrate your fiftieth anniversary on the family yacht.

This crowning achievement would mean you've won at the Shiny Item Collection Game, the Social Media Popularity Game, and the Sneaky Ninja Mom Battle. You turn into solid gold if this level is achieved.

I'm serious. We'll set you on a shelf in a museum somewhere and celebrate your fabulousness.

Now let's discuss another level of insanity, one I'm completely guilty of—assessing which of my classmates from high school look older than I do. I don't even mean to do it! I just see their posts and think, "Hey, I'm thinner/less gray/less wrinkly than she is!" I'm a total idiot, I realize. I'm not proud of this instinct. Let's stop the lunacy right now, shall we? Why are we bothering to compete with each other in these petty ways? I don't even think we know. I think we do it without even trying.

It might be helpful if we reframed the issue and took ourselves right out of the competition. If we've chosen to follow Christ, this means we have a whole new goal in life, and it's not to beat our fellow sisters in a secular game anymore. The shiny things, status, and perfect family have no hold on us anymore, because we understand our place in an eternal kingdom. Everything we see here is about to pass away, because we have a firm grasp on what will come and what will never fade. But what do we do about that? How do we live that out?

> If we've chosen to follow Christ, this means we have a whole new goal in life, and it's not to beat our fellow sisters in a secular game.

Let's refocus. I know almost nothing about professional or Olympic level athletics, other than that those ladies look much nicer in a leotard than I do. But leotards aside, I also know they spend hours perfecting their focus. A gymnast can't be thinking about boys and pizza while she's in the middle of her floor routine. A downhill skier can't be thinking about refinancing her mortgage, because her survival requires absolute focus on the terrain in front of her. One wrong move and she's face-planting into a tree. She can worry about the mortgage situation later, when she's back in the lodge with her cocoa or protein powder or whatever those people drink.

This is why the apostle Paul set his past firmly in the past and focused only on what awaited him. Philippians 3:13–14 tells us that he pressed on to reach the end of his race to receive his heavenly reward after glorifying Jesus Christ. If he'd spent too much time comparing himself to other Christians, he would have lost his nerve. He was the definite loser when it came to Past Holiness Awards, what with his killing the saints and all. Paul's focus on the here and now was in the right place.

There's another story I have highlighted in my Bible, found in 2 Chronicles 20. All the towns of Judah were in trouble because at least three enemy armies were advancing on them. They'd declared war, in fact. Jehoshaphat was terrified because, as leader of Judah, he wasn't sure what to do about three enemy armies breathing down his neck. He became profoundly terrified, then moved through his fear to do something useful about the upcoming problem. He could have gone to the enemies and negotiated a peace agreement, but he didn't focus on human wisdom. He could have run and hidden in a cave, but he didn't trust in his own plans.

Jehoshaphat went right to the Lord and begged for help. And then he ordered the people to begin fasting, which meant that soon everyone was focused on the Lord together. Being hungry has a way of centering your attention pretty directly, I've learned. Together they asked for some big help in this violent competition. They reminded God of his faithfulness and past plans, and asked for help right now. They knew, as a small nation, that their collective goose was cooked. They were about to get decimated. The "vast army from Edom" was marching against them, and things looked grim.

Unless God stepped in for them, of course. As God's people, they recognized they were unable to play the secular game the enemy armies were playing. But the battle of supremacy didn't matter at all to them; they knew they served the all-powerful Yahweh. All the men of Judah stood before the Lord with their little ones, wives, and children, and then the Spirit of the Lord came upon one of the men. He began to prophesy, and this is the message he delivered:

"Listen, all you people of Judah and Jerusalem! Listen, King Jehoshaphat! This is what the LORD says: Do not be afraid! Don't be discouraged by this mighty army, for the battle is not yours, but God's. Tomorrow, march out against them. You will find them coming up through the ascent of Ziz at the end of the valley that opens into the wilderness of Jeruel. But you will not even need to fight. Take your positions; then stand still and watch the LORD's victory. He is with you, O people of Judah and Jerusalem. Do not be afraid or discouraged. Go out against them tomorrow, for the LORD is with you!" (2 Chron. 20:15–17)

Let me emphasize part of that message again: *you will not even need to fight.* Take your positions and just stand there, my people.

Just stand there and wait for his deliverance. When we're engaged in God's game, there's no pressure. There's no competition, because we're about to win. Are we God's people? Then let's act like it. Let's take ourselves out of the silly battles over material possessions or worldly success. Let's watch and learn and maybe laugh a little, when we realize how silly competing over the wrong things can be.

When I turned thirty, which was an entire decade ago, I gave myself a special gift. It was permission to never again play a game of volleyball. I hate volleyball, because it's a terrible combination of individual pressure in a team setting. Is the ball coming at me? Yes, probably. Am I going to be able to do the right thing with it? Never. I always made a terrible mess of things and we lost.

I couldn't stand the pressure anymore, and then one day I realized that, as a game, it was supposed to be fun. No one required me to play volleyball. My status as a wife or mother didn't depend on me doing that ever again.

So, I took myself straight out of the game. I threw up my hands, yelled, "Done!" and never again entered a court. The next time you're listening to a friend set up a "friendly" match of the Shiny Item Collection Game, smile politely. But inside you can yell, "Done!" and walk yourself right out off the field. It's not your competition. You don't have to play anymore. Instead, you can murmur gentle things at your friend that might sound like you're listening, but in fact you'll be looking for an exit for the conversation. As soon as you can reroute her, do it. Take her off the field too. She'll catch on, eventually. At the very least she'll be forced to go find new competitors, which will leave you with some blessed free time.

Make It Personal

1. What competition always leaves you feeling insecure and terrible? How can you take yourself out of it?
2. How do you look in a leotard? Like a fifteen-year-old gymnast, or a forty-year-old matron who's already had a few babies? How do you handle those feelings?

Scripture Focus

"'Listen to me, all you people of Judah and Jerusalem! Believe in the LORD your God, and you will be able to stand firm. Believe in his prophets, and you will succeed.' After consulting the people, the king appointed singers to walk ahead of the army, singing to the LORD and praising him for his holy splendor. This is what they sang: 'Give thanks to the LORD; his faithful love endures forever!' At the very moment they began to sing and give praise, the LORD caused the armies of Ammon, Moab, and Mount Seir to start fighting among themselves" (2 Chron. 20:20–22).

A Prayer for Today

Father, I'm tired of the comparisons and games. I ask that you'll help me focus on your eternal kingdom, not this silly stuff that will fade away. May I love the people around me and trust in you, not compete over what doesn't matter. Amen.

The Day My Daughter Asked for Her Own Bathroom

On Entitlement

PERHAPS I READ too much *Little House on the Prairie* in my formative years, but I don't think every member of the family deserves, by right of their existence on the earth, to have their own bathroom. Call me crazy, but for all the years since time began, humans have been sharing. Sharing space, food, resources, and, yes—even toilet facilities. Therefore and thus, you can imagine how modern American culture rubs me raw nearly every day.

You can further imagine my emotions the day my daughter, a human being I brought into the world and then raised minute-by-minute for thirteen years, came to me and basically demanded her own bathroom. It was a statement, not a polite request.

Now, I think what she was trying to say was, "Mother, my little sibling is a young male, and his portion of the species is lacking in hygiene care and consideration when sharing personal space." She would not have been wrong.

But what I heard was . . . well, nothing. I think I blacked out. My eyes went dark and the only thing I could hear was the rushing in my ears that sounded suspiciously like the word FAILURE screamed over and over again. I'm not even joking. If my kids grow up to feel like their every comfort and whim must be coddled, may a high-speed train jump the tracks and take me right to glory. I will survive the train better than the failure of raising selfish, entitled children. I just cannot have that horsecrappery, as Jen Hatmaker often says.

Yesterday at the orthodontist's office, an SUV pulled into the parking lot just ahead of us. It was the size of a living room. It had pimped-out wheels. It had chrome trim in places I didn't even know an SUV could have trim. It must have cost more than my first house. A tall, skinny blond kid hopped out the passenger's door and skittered into the office before the SUV drove off. Everyone in my family curled up our lips in distaste at his vehicle. Reverse snobbery, if you will. (So maybe I'm not completely failing in the parenting department. Or wait; maybe I'm still totally failing because reverse snobbery is still snobbery. I can't win here!) An hour later the SUV returned and a skinny blond woman in yoga pants darted out like a nervous bird into the waiting area, then zipped back out to wait in her luxurious, chrome-plated tank when it became obvious her son wasn't ready yet. I quickly assumed she couldn't be bothered to wait in the same room as the common peasants.

However, something about her stance and the look on her face gave me pause in the middle of my terrible judgments, and I remembered some grace for just a split second. For all I know, she could have been on her way to the hospital because a loved one was ill. Maybe she was in a hurry for a good reason. Maybe she'd been crying all afternoon and didn't want to weep in the waiting room. Their family might have been drowning in debt or having colossal family fights. Maybe she was about to lose her job or had a kid on drugs.

I decided that a desire to be alone in her huge vehicle couldn't make her a terrible person. I could very well be missing some key information, if the look on her face meant anything.

I decided that if I really wanted to know more about her, I'd have to follow her home to see if they live in a house large enough for everyone to have their own bathroom. Since that would have been weird and quite close to stalking, I decided to let it go. And, you know, write them into a chapter of a book. (That's what you get, America, for living life right in front of writers. You're going to get written into the book. I do not apologize for this.)

I don't know why this family's financial choices bothered me so much. I don't know why entitlement stresses me out so badly, and for all I know, it may not bother you at all. Maybe this chapter is just for me. Fine. I still have some things that need to be said. I just don't think that the culture of Me, Me, Me and Mine, Mine, Mine is sustainable. Families and cultures have always survived by giving and sharing. But we've moved far beyond survival and basic comfort to this insane demand for personal rights that has nothing to do with actual rights.

This is a list of what I think we are entitled to have. I'm sure I've forgotten something, but let's begin with:

Clean, warm, safe shelter.
Some furniture and basic housewares, enough for the family and guests.
Several pairs of underpants. A few bras, if your body comes with a bosom.
Clothes and shoes, but only just enough. Think 1880, not the bulging monstrosity of a closet situation we have now.
A personal toothbrush. Everyone on earth should get their very own, and never have to share this item. Also, a few other basic hygiene items, like deodorant and a comb.
Healthy food.
Clean water for drinking, bathing, and washing clothes.
An education and enough books to fill all the walls of your house.

Clearly no one is going to put me in charge of the world anytime soon, because I've just set standards that would make a Puritan clap for glee. I'm not against fun, I swear. I love fun. I love to eat out and window shop and travel. I don't stay home in a gloomy cloud, wishing despair on the world. But I will sit right here and state that this current rate of consumption is not going to be sustainable. We've created insane levels of debt to finance our demands, both nationally and personally, and one day our houses of cards are going to tumble. And I think that this level of materialism is causing us more stress, not helping us feel better.

Do you remember how houses used to be small, families had one car, and a master's degree wasn't expected for the clerk at the bookshop? It's because people bought what they could afford with money they had, not with what they could borrow. They didn't assume they had to have five bathrooms and an advanced education. What concerns me the most is how little anyone thinks of this anymore. We don't stop to consider what we take for granted, or our slowly creeping standards.

My kids and I were poking around at an estate sale recently, and I fell immediately and deeply in love with the home's 1950s-style stove and oven. They were both pink. Glorious, *I Love Lucy* pink. The kitchen in that house was small enough that a cook could stand in the middle of the room and reach the fridge and the oven at the same time, and they were on opposite sides. My daughter looked at me and said, "Mom, could you even cook in this kitchen? It's so small." I tore my thoughts off the luscious pink oven long enough to say, "Babe, someone's obviously been cooking in here for sixty years. It's totally possible, just not what we're used to."

This doesn't make us bad people, just clueless people. And again, I understand that the bulk of America isn't at all bothered with these new standards. They aren't stressed out by what they don't know.

But do you know who is stressed out by it? Those who don't get to share in the bounty. There are so many, invisibly living right among us, who are getting left out. We're just too busy adding things to our piles that we don't notice them, silently moving in the shadows. What about the poor in our community? What about our churches, silently groaning under the lack of funding?

I just prepared the Mission News for the church where I work. The monthly newsletter had pleas from four missions, all barely squeaking by in their finances. Then the school we support in Haiti sent out a

letter, politely inquiring if they might bother us for an additional five
dollars per month for our sponsored child, as the current twenty-five
dollars per month isn't meeting basic costs.

That's it. That's all they asked for—five measly dollars. Our entitlement isn't stressing us out at all, because the poor and the needy are
bearing that burden for us. Lord, forgive us.

We serve a God who has flagrantly, generously, lavishly given from
the very beginning. The very world he created for us can't even be cata-
logued with his richness and variety and glory. He gave us families and
ways to support our children. We get sweet corn and coffee and sunsets,
butterflies and fireflies and even those giant green caterpillars that turn
into luna moths. He gives and gives and gives. And then he gave us his
Word and his very own Son, so that we could know him better. We
didn't learn this selfish tendency to hoard from our heavenly Father,
that's for certain.

Right from the beginning of history, God taught his people about
giving. He taught about sacrifices and providing for the poor. The first
temple was built from generous offerings of the Israelites, and then Jesus
came and gave his own body. We're supposed to follow this lead, generously sharing all we have. It's an act of worship. Paul reminds us of this
in 2 Corinthians 9:10–11: "For God is the one who provides seed for
the farmer and then bread to eat. In the same way, he will provide and
increase your resources and then produce a great harvest of generosity
in you. Yes, you will be enriched in every way so that you can always be
generous. And when we take your gifts to those who need them, they
will thank God."

See what I mean? Lavish. He spoils us, but we're not supposed to
spoil ourselves. Our bounty is supposed to overflow to others, not sit
in our accounts and gather a toxic mold. Not spill from our closets and
garages and storage units, a testament to how much we hoarded for
ourselves.

The good news here is that I think we can change. In fact, I *know* we
can change. So often we're guilty of making wrong decisions because

we just don't know any better. But I've seen my sisters in action when they realize what's going on outside their own little walls. I've seen us mobilize for the poor, the trafficked, and the lost. The momentum is building as we take stock of reality, pick a passion (because no one can fix all the problems), and get involved. We're getting involved with our time, our resources, our social media posts, and our finances.

We understand that we reap what we sow, and we're ready to sow something far more lasting and far more important than another pair of boots or curtains.

> We understand that we reap what we sow, and we're ready to sow something far more lasting and far more important than another pair of boots or curtains.

A check for the child we support in Haiti is sitting on our kitchen counter. Tomorrow we're going to write our annual letter to him, telling him all about our family and what we're doing right now. If the translation he gets is anything like the translated letter we get from him, he will probably just end up confused and giggling a little bit because things get lost between our cultures. But a photograph of his beautiful, brown, smiling face hangs in our kitchen, right by our dining room table. Caleb prays for him at dinner year-round, beseeching the Lord for a good school year in Haiti. This week Audrey hissed, "It's summer. He's not in school right now," in the middle of the prayer, and then Caleb sighed and amended his prayer that Rodney, no matter what he's doing, would have a good time.

So, we're making some progress. Yes, our kids think kitchens from 1950 are completely unusable and sometimes they demand their own restroom and grooming space. But they also have the beginning inklings of an entire world, right outside this little plastic subdivision. They're starting to understand the bounty we have, and how God never intended for it to get lost in the bowels of this family.

We get it, we give it, we use it, we spread it around. And may we not stop until everyone has their own toothbrush and shelf of books they can read in their own comfy little houses.

Make It Personal

1. How does entitlement show up in your life?
2. What ministries are you passionate about? Why?

Scripture Focus

"Remember this—a farmer who plants only a few seeds will get a small crop. But the one who plants generously will get a generous crop. You must each decide in your heart how much to give. And don't give reluctantly or in response to pressure. 'For God loves a person who gives cheerfully.' And God will generously provide all you need. Then you will always have everything you need and plenty left over to share with others" (2 Cor. 9:6–8).

A Prayer for Today

Heavenly Father, I thank you for all you've given to us. I thank you for the sun, the seasons, and the rain and snow. I thank you for beaches and mountains and forests. I thank you for the people in my life and the gift of your Son. I don't deserve any of your generosity, but I am so grateful for it. Father, please teach me to be a giver, like you are a giver. Amen.

This House Feels Mighty Small at the Moment

On Family Dynamics

ONE THING ALWAYS leads to another. I started out as a young mom on a budget, desperate to make good life choices with the meager resources we had. I began to study budgets, then frugal living, then simple living. Then, somehow, I found my father's stash of *Mother Earth News* magazines, and I realized there was still a whole culture of leftover hippies, living off the grid in debt-free, passively-heated houses.

Soon I was dreaming of living in a rough-hewn log cabin with a composting toilet in the middle of a field. There may have also been a flock of goats in this vision.

And then it got worse. I stumbled onto tiny houses and really lost my mind. I began a crusade to talk my family into moving into one. Then, HGTV thoughtfully supplied me with a series of like-minded lunatics who were doing exactly that. We live about an hour north of a small Amish community where craftsmen make little cottages. They have about ten model homes sitting on a lot, sort of like a car lot for houses, and I drag my family through every house at least once a year. Everyone puts up with it in good humor, knowing Eric will never actually let us sell everything and move into one.

On a cold winter's night last year, I had Caleb do a little experiment with me in the downstairs living room as I examined a tiny-house floor plan from a magazine. We moved all the furniture out of the way and used jump ropes and laundry baskets to mark out a rough approximation of that house. (The entire floor plan took up half of the room!) The problems quickly became apparent. First of all, the bathroom was unworkable. Knees smashed into the wall when a person sat on the pretend toilet. The kitchen was one step from insanity unless we wanted to eat out for every meal for the rest of our lives. And there was absolutely nowhere for four people to go for any kind of privacy whatsoever. It would only work if every member of the family got their own tiny house, and at fifty thousand dollars each, it's more financially responsible to stay in this real house with a real foundation and two real toilets. So there went the tiny house idea.

I had to face reality. I love, and I mean absolutely adore, small houses. I think they're perfect and adorable and easy to maintain and heat—in theory. This theory is a close cousin to my organic-goat-farming, composting-toilet, off-the-grid dream.

But reality proves there is a point where I cannot bear to have one more human in my personal space in any given day. At this very moment, my kids are somewhere downstairs. I should care where, but I don't. I just don't, okay? I can hear Caleb humming a little song, which means he's probably taking advantage of my writing time by playing video games again. This is probably his fourth hour of screen time today, but it's August, and I just avert my eyes and try to get through the end of summer without bloodshed, year after year. Our daughter is probably in her bedroom watching YouTube videos or napping, whatever thirteen-year-olds do after they've been babysitting all day long. Fine. Whatever. I hope she has a nice rest.

In a smaller house we'd all be stuck in the same few small rooms together, all the time. August would find me with crazy eyes and a twitch. I know this for a fact—we used to live in a much smaller house, and there were shoes and flip-flops and balls and kids and cousins and dishes and stuffed animals and blanket forts all over the place. If you think this sounds cozy and delightful, you are correct. It was those things. It was also suffocating when the days got long. Our current house has a whole room for blanket forts and video games and children. It's called the downstairs family room, and I will not apologize for it. Sanity in a floor plan, my friends. I know a tiny house would take away my precious bits of sanity after the fun wore off.

All I'm saying is that family is wonderful, but family with a little bit of breathing room is glorious. These are the people with access to our toothbrushes and food and personal space. They don't always use their access wisely. We're constantly dealing with each other's moods and whims and desires. It's a recipe for disaster, for sure. If everyone could just be endlessly considerate, healthy, and productively occupied, then all would be well. I've never met a family like that, but I'm sure one exists somewhere in the world. Not here, but somewhere.

One of the things I love about the Bible is that it never sugarcoats how difficult family life can be. It fully acknowledges how messy things really are. Time began, and quite shortly thereafter, so did the family dynamics. And by "family dynamics" I mean murders, fights, bad feelings, and snark. The following stories from the book of Genesis show what I mean.

> One of the things I love about the Bible is that it never sugarcoats how difficult family life can be.

Cain killed Abel. Cain felt badly about how his brother's sacrifice was accepted and his own was rejected, so he responded by killing Abel. We've only gotten to the fourth chapter of the Bible and already a brother is down. (See Gen. 4:4–8.)

Noah and his sons had a little issue involving nakedness, drunkenness, and a tent. I won't pretend to understand Noah's rage at his son Ham, but it was severe enough that he cursed Ham's son and blessed Ham's brothers. (See Gen. 9:18–25.)

Lot's daughters both got him drunk and then got pregnant by him, which is, quite frankly, a family problem that goes way beyond "dynamics." The Bible gets weird, man. Gross. (See Gen. 19:30–36.)

Ishmael and Isaac, half brothers and sons of Abraham, squabbled and enraged Isaac's mother so badly that she had Ishmael and his mother sent away. Poor Abraham had to evict part of his family, knowing they'd wander aimlessly in the desert. (See Gen. 21:9–14; 25:18.)

Twins Jacob and Esau couldn't even get along in the womb, let alone a small house. The struggle didn't end at birth, because those two fought for supremacy, snatching blessings and running away, for decades. (See Gen. 25:29–34.)

Joseph and his brothers had so many problems that they threw Joseph into a pit and then sold him into slavery just so they could get rid of him. To be fair, the twerp had lorded his favored status over them for a few years, so he wasn't exactly an innocent party. (See Gen. 37.)

All this from one book in the Bible, and I only included conflict between direct family members. I ignored warring uncles and nephews, battling tribes, and sister wives.

Each of these stories could have been rewritten with the addition of some grace and kindness toward one another. What would have happened if Cain and Abel had a little meeting where they collaborated on a sacrifice? Perhaps Abel could have gently shown his brother a better approach to God, and maybe they could have happily grown old together. Perhaps Ishmael shouldn't have taunted Isaac in the first place, and, of course, maybe Abraham could have not slept with his wife's maid. If he'd trusted God's promise instead of running plan B for God, things would have turned out completely differently. If Joseph hadn't lorded the fancy coat and his father's love over his brothers, maybe they wouldn't have wanted to kill him to shut him up.

A little kindness and consideration goes a long way in a family. Grace extinguishes a multitude of bad feelings and shortcomings if we're willing to offer up love instead of anger and pride. Gentleness, generosity, and fun all belong first *in our homes*, with the people who are closest to us. Sometimes I think we reserve those things for the outside world and leave our families with all of our grossness.

Do the people in our homes get our best behavior? Or do they get our personal book of the Genesis conflict? There's a reason the Bible exhorts us to be concerned with not only our own good but the good of others. Our freedom in Christ gives us a lot of room and flexibility, but we're called to always have an eye on how our choices affect our loved ones. We're told to get rid of all our bitterness and harsh words and to replace them with kindness and tenderheartedness. Ephesians 4:32 says to "be kind to each other, tenderhearted, forgiving one another, just as God through Christ has forgiven you." We're called to forgive like Christ forgave us, not to harass our family members until they do something drastic and end up on the evening news. Or in the book of Genesis, even.

We're also told to build one another up and to encourage one another. I completely understand how hard this can be in a family setting. Sometimes our loved ones' quirks can literally wear grooves into our nerves. If you wear a groove into a thing long enough, you're going to mark it permanently. It can be hard to get out of that pattern and start new, healthy interactions. But the alternative is exactly what happened to the biblical families we mentioned above. Do we really want our own legacies marked with battles, murders, and hatred? NO. No, we do not. We want better for our families, and it's often up to us to start a new trend of forgiveness, kindness, and grace.

I have all faith that we can do it. I know we can change the atmosphere in our homes and families and change our futures at the same time.

One of the definitions of grace is "undeserved favor." It's not easy to respond with kindness when the kids won't get ready and cause us to be late for an appointment, or when the husband forgets to tell us he's leaving for a hunting weekend with the boys. When our daughters have their own PMS raging and they're acting like the teenagers we used to be, when our sons' bedrooms smell like fetid swamps boiling with dirty clothes and sports equipment, and on the days when we can't even stand ourselves, our homes need undeserved favor. If we give everyone in our family exactly what they deserve, then we're going down in a biblical debacle. It's going to happen to us too.

The whole beautiful thing about Christ is that he came for us when we least deserved it. He rewrote our life story with his grace, offering us life and peace and unity with God when we deserved to roam the desert without him for eternity. We deserve the stinking sewer we created for ourselves, but he lifted us out of it.

I love to imagine what will happen in our families when we decide to follow Christ's example. He could turn our sewers into clean, safe places of his blessing. We could watch as anger and bitterness melt into caring and gentleness, aimed at every person in our home. Small homes might begin to feel cozy and delightful, instead of loaded with toxins.

I'm still totally up for the idea of a tiny house one day. I think it could work when it's just Eric and me all by ourselves again. So, when our kids head to college, we might be in the market for our own tiny utopia. Until then, you'll find us in this normal American home, creatively avoiding each other until school starts again. There will be grace and kindness, but there will also be personal space. Amen.

Make It Personal

1. How much room do you think the ideal home has for your family?
2. What could grace heal in your family? What things can you do today to give your family grace?

Scripture Focus

"For God chose to save us through our Lord Jesus Christ, not to pour out his anger on us. Christ died for us so that, whether we are dead or alive when he returns, we can live with him forever. So encourage each other and build each other up, just as you are already doing" (1 Thess. 5:9–11).

For further study, read 1 Corinthians 10:23–24.

A Prayer for Today

Heavenly Father, I thank you for this home and the people who fill its space each day. Family life is messy and hard, and I am grateful your Word doesn't deny that fact. Please walk with us, moment by moment, and teach us how to treat each other well in the smallest of ways. Please turn the tide of bitterness and harsh words. May we gradually become more and more like you, full of grace and gentleness. Amen.

When Thanksgiving Includes a Table for Ninety-Eight

On Family Dynamics, Extended Edition

LISTEN.

People are weirdos.

And sometimes those weirdos end up at your holiday table. Let's just accept that we can watch Martha Stewart create beautiful holiday tables with her natural grasses and subtle sequins for six solid hours, but our table will never look like her table because her photographs leave out all the weirdos who end up at your place.

Uncle Steve with his cigar and flask? At your table.

Aunt Peggy with the organic wool underwear and the essential oil therapy? Next to Uncle Steve.

Thirty small, squealing children? And two of them are hiding under the table and sneaking Jell-O, slowly grinding it into your carpet? Yes, exactly those. The other twenty-eight are loose somewhere in your house, and good luck getting them all out at the end of the day. You'll be finding stray short people for a week, eating pudding in your attic and wearing your husband's shoes. The kids, not you.

Let's not forget the grandparents, siblings, cousins, kids home from college, next-door neighbors, and of course your own immediate family. They're all coming. Get the biggest turkey, sister.

For the purpose of this chapter, we're defining family as anyone who could show up at your special event, due to any combination of genetics, legal relationship, or personal history. Whoever these weirdos are, they're yours to keep. Yours to feed, house, and shoo out at the end of a very taxing day. They may have stressed you out for decades, but this year is going to be different. I'm here to help you, and this year you'll have perfect harmony when the family comes to visit.

Just kidding. I'm a writer, not a miracle worker. Family is nuts and there's no such thing as perfect harmony whenever relatives are involved. Did you just read the last chapter? Those families were killing each other and dropping brothers into pits! Let's aim for a family experience that ends better than Joseph's pit thing, okay? I feel that's more reasonable. I think we can manage that together this year.

> Let's aim for a family experience that ends better than Joseph's pit thing, okay?

Of course, I don't even know what family experience you're trying to weather. Maybe the obvious ones like Thanksgiving and Christmas are coming to mind. But you could also be dreading a wedding, family reunion, or the annual Fourth of July celebration. Maybe you'll be in sweaters and wool suits, or maybe you'll be in flip-flops and tank tops. I don't know if you'll be sitting down to a formal meal or grabbing a hot dog as the parade shuffles past.

What I do know is that this accumulation of quirky folks is a potent cocktail of chaos. It doesn't matter what the specific holiday is; what matters is that all these people are going to be in one place for a good, long time. As I write this, my own sister's wedding is two weeks away. I don't have a dress. I don't have shoes. I know my nails won't be long enough to look decent by then, and mostly I'm hyper-focusing on these little details because these special events throw our family's dynamics right out the window and I'm too nervous about what might happen on her big day.

Our father is most comfortable at home, on his farm, dressed in retired-man pants. He has a few sweatshirts that our mom threatens to throw out at least once a week, and he wears them in a steady rotation. This is the man who just got fitted for a new suit last week, and he's actually going to be wearing it. Mom spends her days futzing around the house and going out with her best friend to see Melissa McCarthy movies. My brother and his wife live in Detroit with their giant dog, Moose. But two weeks from today we're all going to be putting on our fancy clothes (assuming I can find something to wear) and gathering at a nice place where we have to be on our best behavior for hours.

It's not that we have bad social skills; it's just that we're best at home where we can nap and read and such when we run out of our social skills.

I should probably mention that my sister, the radiant bride, is also going around the bend. She's not looking forward to having everyone stare at her for the whole night, and she's keenly aware of how hard it is to keep a hundred people happy for an entire evening. This says a lot about her, that she even cares if everyone is happy for her entire wedding. She does. She really does care. But a hundred people come with a hundred viewpoints, and that's about ninety-nine more than she can handle in any given situation.

Oh, and one more thing—this summer has been boiling hot by Michigan standards, and the ceremony is outside. This means we might be sweating through our fancy clothes if the evening is ninety-three degrees like last night. There's a very good chance I'm about to be a sweaty, plump sister with short nails and uncomfortable shoes on the porch of the reception hall.

Lord, hear my prayer. May we not implode from the social pressure to maintain dignity when we really just want a nap and a cool cloth on our faces.

It's not that I'm dreading the wedding; it's just that I can see where things could go so badly wrong. But don't worry; I'm not saying a word to Beth. By the time you read this, the big day will be long past and my sister and her husband will have settled into normal life that doesn't involve fancy dresses or sweaty weirdos at the fancy buffet.

The wedding may soon be over and the holiday may pass, but we can't escape the weirdos entirely. They'll always be among us. I think even Jesus knew that. No, wait. Technically I think he mentioned that the *poor* will always be among us, but do you know what Jesus was? A weirdo! A total misfit! He entered the scene in the middle of generations of religious rule and blew it all asunder. He came with love for people, with a strange perception of the kingdom, with healing, and with a disregard for rules. The Gospels are full of examples of when he sat down for a meal and upset the Pharisees because he couldn't play nicely and stick to the polite script they wanted to hear from him.

After he was crucified, the Pharisees thought they finally had disposed of this traveling, teaching weirdo. Then Paul entered the scene. Do you know what Paul was? Another weirdo. Couldn't keep his mouth shut. Filled with passion and fire, at first he traveled around keeping the very establishment Jesus denied alive, and then he switched sides and decided Jesus was the right way, after all. He then spent the rest of his life pointing straight back to Jesus, no matter what beatings or shipwrecks he had to endure. He could have just stayed home and stayed quiet and saved everyone a lot of grief.

I remind myself of these two guys whenever I wish the holidays involved a few polite hugs, a pleasant dinner, and then naps around the Christmas tree. Sometimes the misfits make us uncomfortable, but they might be the ones we need at the table the most.

I know some of you are considering your Uncle Steve. You're comparing him to the Messiah and you're calling my bluff. You're thinking, *No. Not the same. I will not be convinced.*

I concede your point. I've got a few of those relatives too, but they won't be reading this book, so I think it's safe to admit that in print. Let's assume, for the sake of truth, that we all have some misfit relatives that we must endure but who bear no resemblance at all to Jesus or Paul. They're just quirky, imperfect individuals who will be gracing our table for a lengthy time soon.

In these situations, I think we can only accept the differences and the quirks. I know it's hard. I get that they're driving you crazy. I understand. I have hidden in my bathroom before too. I've also hidden in the downstairs closet, the garage, and the store, because we "ran out of something."

That "something" may have been an industrial-sized bag of chocolate and noise-cancelling headphones, but that's another discussion for another time.

When we experience friction with close family members who constantly share our space, we can set up rules and boundaries. We know we'll lose it every once in a while, but we also know we have years to average out our foibles and shortcomings. For holiday guests, the rules are a little different. Special occasions come as intense, short bursts. We don't have the same advantage of time. We don't have months and years; we have seconds and minutes. Like machine-gun fire, once a year.

For this, we grit our teeth and choose to be flexible. We choose to accept differences and be content with the fact that our family members are who they are. We aren't going to change them. They aren't looking for our approval; they're looking for pumpkin pie and a football game. They don't care how many hours we spent on the decorations or the turkey; they just want a safe place to put the baby down while they talk to other adults. They might need a comfortable chair for their old bones, or a big glass of water for their back pills.

See? What are we so worried about? It's all fine. There's nothing here that can't be fixed with a little flexibility and kindness, right? Among Christians, everyone gets a place. Everyone gets a seat. Weirdo or not.

> Among Christians, everyone gets a place.
> Everyone gets a seat. Weirdo or not.

If we're talking about non-Christian relatives, then we are literally representing Christ to them. The stakes suddenly spike very high. They might not be in church for a sermon this Sunday, so what they see in us as we scoop the mashed potatoes and burn the rolls is all they'll know.

If our God is generous, may our servings be heaping. If our God is kind, then may we gently pull the rascals from under the table and not yell too loudly about the Jell-O issue there. If our Jesus was all about love, then may our words and attitudes be soaked with that same love.

We may be the only thing they know about God, and may we represent our Lord well. Paul, that same misfit we just talked about, understood our responsibility here. He worked hard to convince others of Christ, and he asked the early church to follow suit. Christ's love controlled him, and because he believed Christ had died for him, he would also die to his own life. The old annoyances and fights died too. He lived not for himself but for Christ. And then he considered himself an ambassador for Jesus, pleading with others to come to God.

Ambassadors don't go to another country to convince the citizens to become something they're not. They just go with a message, content to allow those individuals to be whoever they're going to be. Stinky cigars, essential oils, and crying babies are all fine. Ambassadors don't get hung up on the personality quirks or social gaffes. They just keep saying what they're sent to say, repeat and repeat, until hopefully one day someone catches the message.

I think it's time to insert a little side note here. So far in this conversation, I've assumed that your loved ones are difficult to be around, but not actually dangerous. I'm working under the assumption that your relationships with them make you roll your eyes, but aren't abusive. But those assumptions might be naive. I would never want you to put yourself or your children at risk because you feel that, because of Jesus, you must put up with any behavior they choose. Please be wise. There are some situations that need to be resolved from a distance, or may not be resolved at all. If your family gathering is a violent, alcohol-soaked event, it's okay to steer clear.

If you can find a way to love your family members at other times or in other ways, great. We have a friend who will agree to meet his mother at a restaurant for brunch once or twice a year, but will not take his children to her home. He's striving for a balance of love and healthy boundaries, but is totally unwilling to expose his kids to his mother's poor choices and unstable lifestyle. He prays, and then uses discretion.

And also, for the most serious cases, don't hesitate to involve the authorities if need be. Please don't think protecting a family member from the consequences of their own abusive choices is what God would have you do. It's not. Romans 13:1 says, "Everyone must submit to governing authorities. For all authority comes from God, and those in positions of authority have been placed there by God." If you suspect an uncle has been sexually abusing a child, go to the police. It might feel like an ambassador of Jesus might not want an relative to go to jail, but our authorities say abuse is an action worthy of incarceration. Err on the side of protecting the innocent and vulnerable.

Sometimes love is tough. Be careful. Be wise. Seek mature counsel if you need it.

So, back to the eye-rolling, grit-your-teeth kind of relationships. The relative who makes you rub your temples and pray for patience is bound to be in your personal space soon. May we be ambassadors of our God's love and grace. May we go forth with mashed potatoes or hot dogs. Fancy heels and a wedding dress or flip flops and a sweaty tank top. The details don't matter, but loving our family in spite of their quirks matters quite a lot.

We can do it, because we can survive most anything for an afternoon, right?

No, seriously. Right?

Make It Personal

1. What's the best and worst example of family time you've experienced?
2. Think of the one family member who pushes you over the edge, and proactively think of ways to handle it better this year.

Scripture Focus

"Because we understand our fearful responsibility to the Lord, we work hard to persuade others. God knows we are sincere, and I hope you know this, too. . . . If it seems we are crazy, it is to bring glory to God. And if we are in our right minds, it is for your benefit. Either way, Christ's love controls us. Since we believe that Christ died for all, we also believe that we have all died to our old life. He died for everyone so that those who receive his new life will no longer live for themselves. Instead, they will live for Christ, who died and was raised for them. . . . And he gave us this wonderful message of reconciliation. So we are Christ's ambassadors; God is making his appeal through us. We speak for Christ when we plead, 'Come back to God!'" (2 Cor. 5:11, 13–15, 19–20).

A Prayer for Today

Heavenly Father, I need your help, and I need it in a really specific way. It's almost time to gather with my extended family again, and honestly, Lord . . . we're all just such a mess. Please be with us. Please give us grace and kindness to each other. May I represent you well. If my family doesn't make it into church, may they at least see you in me. I cannot do this alone, because left to myself, I will have a fit and destroy the day over something dumb. Amen.

The Cat and Other Things I Can't Get Rid Of

On Their Things

THE WORST DECISION of my entire life howls at the door every morning after I feed him a breakfast of disgusting, moist food out of a can. He sheds clumps of black hair all over my carpet. He wakes the entire family up in the middle of the night with his shenanigans. He has done unspeakable things with his bodily fluids all over the house.

I hate him so much.

His name is Captain Kitty, and when he's not being an idiot, he's the sweetest, kindest cat you can imagine. I've watched as an exuberant toddler pinned him to the floor and squished him with boundless love, and the beast just let it happen. No howling or scratching or biting, just waiting it out. If there was so much as a stitch of meanness in that cat I would have tossed him out long ago, but his sweetness (more importantly, Eric's sweetness) has saved his hairy black bacon. I recently called Animal Control and spoke to an officer. The conversation went mostly like this:

Me: Sir, before we begin I need to know if you're an animal lover.

Guy: Ma'am, I've been told that, as an animal control officer, I love all animals.

Me: Good. We're on the same page, then. I have a cat and I think I need to have it put down. What do I need to know?

Guy: Is the animal dangerous?

Me: No. Absolutely not. But he's destroying my house. I'm about to have to spend thousands of dollars to replace things where he's peeing and spraying.

Guy: Ah. Well, in that case, we wouldn't even try to adopt him out if we know he's destroying the home. We'd just put him down.

Me: Fine. I can't bear the thought of him being sad and scared at the shelter, but I can totally bear the thought of him going to sleep for eternity with no pain.

Guy: You'll need a driver's license and twenty dollars. That covers it all.

Twenty dollars. My worst decision ever could be rectified with twenty measly bucks? At that point in the morning, I was so enraged at the cat I would have put him in the carrier by myself (a nearly impossible feat for one adult) and paid any sum of money to have my problem disappear. I texted my husband the good news, and he wisely texted back that killing the cat might be detrimental to our children's mental health. They love him. Audrey, in particular, adores him with an unending and infuriating love.

And this is why Captain Kitty still lives here. I love that child of mine, so the cat is here to stay. Last night I was rubbing his furry belly as he slept on his back in the middle of my bed, legs akimbo and aimed at the four corners of the room. "I wish you'd die, you terrible beast," I crooned. Eric laughed but didn't disagree.

The cat is the worst of it, but he's not the only thing I deal with around here. From where I'm sitting I can see two foam swords, a tool set, stacks of books, and toys. If I moved downstairs I would be visually assaulted by craft supplies, clean laundry that hasn't made it to closets, an impressive collection of nail polish, stuffed animals from 2005, and a stack of video games.

Oh, my word. The extra stuff. It suffocates me. I'd throw it all out, except an episode of *Hoarders* still haunts me. The woman had grown up in a military family and every four years they transferred bases. They couldn't move things over a certain weight limit, so her parents threw out all her precious possessions every four years. It had obviously left deep and permanent scars on the poor woman, because she stood sobbing as the dumpster hauler took her adult-sized hoard to the landfill, where it belonged.

At that point, as my mouth hung open and I watched her cry on the screen, I decided I might need to back off a little bit. There's obviously a point where my reaction to their stuff can go too far, can cause too much pain. I may be stressed out by it, but there has to be a better way than emotionally scarring them.

I've tried to handle stress and chaos by scheduling, preparing, and budgeting. I'm that mom who politely refuses to be in the PTA and the band boosters because I know those groups will push past my calendar's limit. I'm a no-no-no and throw-throw-throw kind of woman. When it comes to possessions, if they aren't useful or beautiful or absolutely loved, they're gone. G-O-N-E.

Sometimes Eric finds me standing in the closet, finger to lips, quietly contemplating the contents. "Whatcha doing?" he asks, knowing full well the answer.

"Just checking to make sure we still need all this stuff," I say with my sweetest, not-crazy smile. He backs away slowly, knowing he doesn't actually care if I get rid of the coolers, the folding chairs, or the umbrella. He can live with almost nothing, and he proved it all through college. The man once went camping with a sleeping bag and a toothbrush. For the entire weekend. That's it. He was fine.

I was reading a book by Joshua Becker on minimalism. Titled *The More of Less: Finding the Life You Want Under Everything You Own,* Becker's book talks to minimalists who are trapped in homes with family members of an opposite mind-set. And although the man had just spent 169 pages evangelizing the message of simple living and minimal possessions, he had some strong words to say to people who are stressed out by their loved ones' things—relax, accept your family, and choose peace. Here are Becker's exact words:

> Your relationship with your spouse and children matter so much more than where you are on the road to minimalism.
>
> I have heard from a number of people who have taken steps toward minimalism in their lives but in the process have become so frustrated with their spouses or children that they have allowed stress and resentment to set in. . . .
>
> Realize that you can't change someone else. You can only educate, encourage, and assist, as permitted. . . .
>
> One of the greatest marks of love is patience. When you feel your frustration growing and you are ready to lash out in anger at one of your family members, take a deep breath. Remind yourself that you are not perfect either.[7]

He's right. He's totally right. I know this, and I also know that I'm the one who takes things too far around here. I've been teaching my kids to be tidy since they were toddlers, and Eric is naturally a thoughtful and neat man. I'm not living with an actual problem; I am the problem. What we have here is evidence of a family living a beautiful life, not a cluttered, filthy pile of junk.

As the wife and mother, I set a lot of the attitude and tone of the home. I don't want my kids to grow up with memories of a crazy woman whipping through closets and throwing away stuff in a rage. I don't want them to feel like I'm hunting through the house, waiting to grab a stray toy or doodad just in time for garbage day.

Don't get me wrong; I totally do those things. I just don't want them scarred from the memory. I want people to sit around at my funeral laughing at all the weird stuff I did, not sobbing as a therapist pats their shoulder and hands them a tissue. I want my daughter to one day scrub cat fluids from a carpet and lovingly remember all the times I did the same for her infernal Captain Kitty. And yes, she may be swearing under her breath just like I do, but won't that just build more happy memories for her to pass to her own children?

Yes? Hopefully?

I want to set a tone of peace and acceptance in my home. Sometimes this means averting my eyes and letting the tool kit Caleb got for Christmas sit in the living room. Sometimes it means a Lego project is stored under the ottoman for the entire summer as he slowly works on it. Always it means closing a bedroom door and pretending that whatever's going on in there is fine and wonderful and I don't need to worry my pretty little head about it.

I repeat to myself, "It's fine, it's fine, it's fine. No one from *Hoarders* is going to show up at my door this afternoon, hoping to tape a quick episode."

Maybe you have no idea of what any of this feels like because you've never been a clean freak for a day in your life. Piles of things may bring you comfort. You may be completely overjoyed to sit down with a stack of magazines you saved for two decades, or to show your children every single outfit they wore their first year. You might be stressing out because now you feel bad about your lifestyle and wonder how many friends are silently judging you. But you actually have a lot to offer your neatnik friends, did you know that? Your casual acceptance of your house often means you're willing to throw your doors open at any moment to sit down with a friend. You likely value people and relationships over compulsively getting rid of clutter, and that is something a few of your tidier friends need to see in action. Heaven knows I need to see it. I'm daily brought back to reality when I realize my friends are okay with dirty dishes in the sink or piles of clean laundry on the couch. Call it your Ministry of Dirty Dishes and let it go at that.

Christians are called to set our minds on the important things, and those things are never things. People are important. God is even more important. Loving others and God should never come after a tidy house or some weird standard of organization. We need to focus on God's peace, which is greater than anything we can see or understand. We need that peace to guard our hearts and minds as we choose to live in Christ Jesus.

> Christians are called to set our minds on the important things, and those things are never things.

Colossians 3:12–15 reminds us: "Since God chose you to be the holy people he loves, you must clothe yourselves with tenderhearted mercy, kindness, humility, gentleness, and patience. Make allowance for each other's faults, and forgive anyone who offends you. Remember, the Lord forgave you, so you must forgive others. Above all, clothe yourselves with love, which binds us all together in perfect harmony. And let the peace that comes from Christ rule in your hearts."

So, I can walk around my house fuming at the drum set no one plays and the bin of dress-up clothes no one's used for five years, or I can cool my jets and think about how empty and terrible this house would be if none of these people were here to fill the house with all this stuff. I can think of the refugees across Europe who barely have a pair of shoes and the clothes on their backs. They'd trade places with me in a hot minute.

Don't think I haven't considered boxing up some of this stuff and mailing it right over the great blue sea to them. I surely have. But I don't think that's quite the most efficient way to go about it.

"Turn away from evil and do good. Search for peace, and work to maintain it," the Psalmist tells me (Ps. 34:14). "Better a dry crust eaten in peace than a house filled with feasting—and conflict," Proverbs 17:1 chimes in. These verses are probably better options for handling things at home, choosing peace over my own desires for a clutter-free home.

In this house, I get to help set the attitude and tone, and it begins in my own heart. I earnestly pray that the peace of Christ fills me up, overflows, and then seeps downward onto the physical things we own.

Because I really don't want to see my own kid on *Hoarders* one day, weeping as they clear her home of tons of garbage.

Make It Personal

1. Do you think your family balances tidiness and messiness? What can you do as a group to strike a better balance?
2. How does each member of your family view their personal possessions? (For example, one child I know gives every item a human personality, so he feels very sad if anything gets lost or thrown out.) How can you better love each person while still addressing the items in your home?

Scripture Focus

"Work at living in peace with everyone, and work at living a holy life, for those who are not holy will not see the Lord. Look after each other so that none of you fails to receive the grace of God. Watch out that no poisonous root of bitterness grows up to trouble you, corrupting many" (Heb. 12:14–15).

A Prayer for Today

Heavenly Father, thank you for all these blessings. Please help me to set a tone of peace and acceptance in this home, but please help us to balance our possessions and the need for tidiness. May we always remember there are those who have nothing, and work to meet those needs instead of adding to our piles. Amen.

Part 3

Sometimes I Stress Myself Out

The Stress We Cause Ourselves

THIS IS WHERE stuff gets real, girls. Up to now we've looked outward at all the things that cause us stress, but now we've reached the last frontier of stress. We have to look inward. Because honestly, some of the stress we're experiencing starts right in our own cute little selves.

We can be our own worst enemies, can't we?

There are times when the worst stress is a direct consequence of our choices and human limits. There are times I'm reading the Gospels and I identify so closely with the hard-hearted, close-minded Pharisees. You know, the guys Jesus butted heads with over and over again. *Those* jerks.

I can be that jerk. And when I'm not busy being overly pious and self-righteous, I can mess up the rest of my life by trying to control everything, overscheduling our calendar, and setting unreasonable standards.

And let's not forget the days I nap instead of doing something productive, like writing a book or something. Of course I'm stressed out—I just set an impossible schedule and then procrastinated and didn't get anything done! Madness!

But don't worry. We're not going to finish the book on a gloomy, self-defeating note. We may be a mess, but we're going to have a good time with that mess. What we can deal with, we'll deal with. What we need to turn over to God, we'll turn right over.

And what we need to laugh at and let go, we'll mock relentlessly until it doesn't stress us out anymore, okay?

Okay. Let's get after ourselves for a few minutes, and see how it all works out.

Maybe Tonight a Magic Fairy Will Appear

On Procrastination

HAND TO THE heavens, I had this morning set aside to write this chapter, but instead I spent most of the time making pancakes, drinking coffee in a leisurely fashion, and then ripping out carpet.

I direct you to the chapter titled "The Cat and Other Things I Can't Get Rid Of" for further details on this carpet situation, but let me add that the humidity level today is about 98 percent and the cat odor is about the same. The carpet has to go or we have to set fire to the basement. Those are our options. My husband is at work and when he comes home to what I've done . . . he'll be fine. He's not the one who has to rip out the carpet and figure out what to do with the bare concrete underneath. That's my job.

I know the flooring isn't the most pressing thing on order for this day, because the cat will be wreaking havoc in this house until one of us finally dies, but somehow the idea of dealing with that specific, tangible duty is much more appealing than sitting down at the computer to wrestle with slippery words and vague ideas. I'm stalling until the words pop into my head. It happens like that a lot, where I'll be doing something completely different, my writing mind at rest, and then KABOOM. Words pour in like a faucet turned on somewhere in my left frontal lobe.

I'm waiting for the faucet, you might say. And while I'm waiting, I might do a few other things, like tackle that giant load of laundry that's waiting on the bed for me, weed the flowerbeds, and possibly wax the minivan.

I'm desperate. I need a little writing fairy to show up and help things along. And while she's at it, I hope she brings all of her friends: Magic Dinner Fairy, Ethereal Dust the Baseboards Fairy, and, of course, the Amazing Play Legos for Six Hours with Child Fairy. I've been putting all those things off for a long time too.

I'm not the only one who lets things pile up for way too long, though, so that's a slight comfort. My friends and I give ourselves all kinds of stress because we procrastinate on things like visiting the dentist and getting a mammogram or a colonoscopy. What about exercising or quitting smoking? We avoid those things if possible, simply because we're deeply in denial that the unpleasantness is worth the effort. Why work hard and be miserable if we can be happy while we wait in denial? Why suffer early?

We can't forget about cleaning out the refrigerator, doing the dishes, balancing the checkbook (or the credit and debit card statements), calculating a budget, or saving for retirement, can we? Why do it now? Maybe in a few minutes or days or decades things will be better.

It's time for the cold, hard, terrible truth. *It's not going to be better later.* Procrastinating only lets all the stress pile up behind closed doors, and when we eventually have to open that door and deal with the mess it's going to be one hundred times worse. Dental problems don't magically go away. Diabetes only gets more dangerous the longer we ignore it. That weird noise the van is making is simply an odd sound today, but two days from now the engine might fall right out.

Pretend you open up a jar of sauerkraut and put it back in your cupboard. If you get right back to that jar in a few minutes, everything's fine. You can add it to the sausage in the pan, and dinner is almost done. (Author's note: I don't actually eat sauerkraut. Can't even spell it. It's a horrendous food product. But it was the stinkiest thing I could think of to make my point.) If you wait until the evening, an odd smell is going to be sneaking out of the cupboard cracks. If you ignore the smell and go to bed, in the morning your breakfast is going to be ruined by the stench.

If you go on vacation for a month without dealing with that sauerkraut, when you return you're going to have to burn the house down (like our basement carpet situation) and get a new one.

Sure, fermented cabbage is stinky and sort of gross. But it gets so much worse if we let it rot.

I am here to be the kick in the pants you need to avoid rotted cabbage, my friend, and I need you to return the favor. I need you to get me moving on my writing, my fridge cleanout session, and the new health plan I swear I'll begin each Monday.

But some of you may have a situation that is far too complicated to be fixed by a ridiculous story about sauerkraut. Let's break our approach down into manageable steps. First, let's evaluate whether we have an issue that actually requires our attention right now. Ask yourself these questions: Does this really matter? Does it affect the quality of life for my family, my friends, or myself? Often the answer is no. Then it has the shelf life of a Twinkie. This thing in question could rot in a cupboard for eternity and none will be the wiser. Then fine. Don't do that thing. Let it go and get on to actual items.

For example, let's consider dusting the baseboards and learning to knit. Sure, you could do those things, but a little baseboard dust never killed anyone and the mall sells things that are already knitted for your enjoyment. Done and done. Already you have two less things to worry about.

But there are other things that really do need to get done, and we all know what they are. They vary from woman to woman, but ignoring them is only making things worse. You have your own list of things you don't want to do, and avoiding them is causing a whole new kind of strain.

I think it's time to throw down the Proverbs 31–woman gauntlet.

Yes, I know. If I hear one more Mother's Day sermon where the pastor exhorts this female as the golden standard, I'll tip over and bang my face on the pew in front of me. She exhausts me, but I waited almost twenty chapters to bring her up, so you'll have to excuse me for a moment.

Let's examine her calendar and life choices. She found and spun wool, which sounds to me like she chased down a sheep and then gave it a haircut and then did something useful with that wooly harvest. She brought her food from afar, and I doubt that meant the grocery store on the opposite side of town. She got up early to make sure everyone had a good, hearty breakfast, and then she planned out her servants' daily duties. She inspected a field and bought it, worked hard with those burly arms so prized in ancient cultures (I am making things up again, but it sounds about right), she drove a hard bargain, and then she made her own cloth.

That's enough for now. I'm only halfway through this soliloquy and I can't do it anymore. I'm exhausted and wishing she would sit down and act like a normal person for a while. We get the point, though. Without those specific activities, her household was going to fall apart. They needed clothes and food and structure, and she made sure she was on top of it all. Bless her heart. Procrastination would have meant they all starved or froze and the sheep would have been running rampant, needing haircuts. Her disciplined, timely efforts made a huge difference to her household.

Maybe you really want to be very Proverbs-Thirty-Onely. You'd love to shear the sheep and consider the field. You want your household to run well, but you feel like your entire life is ganging up on you, and you're procrastinating because you don't know where to begin. Hiding is a fair reaction to oppressive situations, and now I've just added Middle Eastern expectations from thousands of years ago to your to-do list.

Let me give us both a little grace—this is just my opinion, and I don't have any hard or fast biblical backing for it—but I wonder if the Proverbs 31 woman is simply a composite of a lot of well-lived women's lives. I don't think God or our families are expecting us to get through all those responsibilities every day. Maybe those ancient women managed those things in seasons, as children were born and then grew up.

It's downright hard to consider a field and then buy it when you're carrying a baby on your hip while your toddler runs rampant through the vineyard, right? Maybe our ancient woman stayed home and kept things slow and easy until the kids were old enough to stay home by themselves for a few hours. There's a profound difference between unhealthy procrastination and adapting to the realities of your season of life, and I don't think the Bible means for us to work ourselves into a holy frenzy. We don't have to do every good thing right now.

> I don't think the Bible means for us to work ourselves into a holy frenzy. We don't have to do every good thing right now.

Reorganizing our to-do list gets easier as we practice evaluating each item. Eventually, we're able to recognize what really needs our attention now and what can wait. We're able to discern what is our job currently, and what will be our job in the next season of our lives.

I wish I had a magic formula to help you with these decisions, but I think the only way to do this is to just jump in, and then listen carefully to your body, your emotional health, and your family as you begin to work through what appears to need attention now. It's a balance—are you more stressed out by things that aren't getting done, or by actually doing the things?

If you're exhausted just getting the basics done, that's okay. Just back off a little on the grand to-do scheme, and do the basics with no guilt until your kids are older or your job is less demanding. If you find yourself sobbing in the shower more than once a week, take notice of that. You're probably doing too much. If your family seems anxious and upset with your new level of activity, then that's a good indicator as well. On the other hand, if your husband claps for glee when he can find matching socks and the bank statements are balanced, then that's good feedback. You're probably on the right track.

The point here is that we want to live our lives well. We need to learn how to give attention and effort to the things that matter, *when* they matter. And if that looks like a little bit of procrastination for now, then fine. We can live with that. You'll know if putting things off is causing you stress or saving your sanity.

Speaking of which, if you'll excuse me, I really need to finish up that carpet work I started earlier today. And if anyone would like to receive a cat in the mail, I would be glad to ship him to you. Immediately.

Make It Personal

1. Read Proverbs 31:10–31 and translate that woman's life into a modern-day equivalent. What parts of her situation make any sense to your life? Are there similarities? Anything you'd like to do as well?
2. That thing you're avoiding—what is it? What do you need to do about it today? Or is it the "Twinkie" in your life and you need to let it sit on the shelf?

Scripture Focus

"Know the state of your flocks, and put your heart into caring for your herds, for riches don't last forever, and the crown might not be passed to the next generation. After the hay is harvested and the new crop appears and the mountain grasses are gathered in, your sheep will provide wool for clothing, and your goats will provide the price of a field. And you will have enough goats' milk for yourself, your family, and your servant girls" (Prov. 27:23–27).

A Prayer for Today

Heavenly Father, I know this procrastination is silly. The longer I put it off, the worse my stress about it grows. But, somehow, I can't seem to gather the courage or the energy to deal with it. I ask for wisdom to know what needs to be done and what really can wait. Then, please help me take the first step. Amen.

You Know What Would Fix This? Doing It My Way.

On Micromanagement

EVERY ONCE IN a while, I suffer from a mild mental lapse in my life choices and find myself chaperoning a middle school dance.

Audrey is our social butterfly, so dances are the most delightful thing she can imagine happening in a school building. She's surrounded by all her friends, plus the lights are low and the music is thumping. She gets two hours to wander through the cafeteria, eating cookies and having a grand old time. She's in her glory.

I grew up in a home where school dances were surely considered a gateway to Satan's playground, so I was never allowed to go. This didn't bother me because I'd far rather be home with a book than in a gym with Bon Jovi blasting through the speakers. I could politely blame my parents and say, "I can't go to the dance; my parents are super strict," and then stay home and read. Win-win!

When our daughter reached middle school and started begging to go to dances, I agreed she could go, but only if I chaperoned. She sighed, agreed to my terms, and then made me promise not to talk to boys on her behalf or do any dancing. With the negotiations settled and both parties satisfied, we set off for the school. That first event felt like I was walking into foreign territory. I set my mind on protecting the innocent middle school students by keeping a close eye out for drugs, alcohol in hidden flasks, or sex in the bathrooms.

I had been there fifteen minutes before I realized I was an idiot. I don't know what goes on at urban schools, but our dances are essentially a two-hour indoor recess with loud music. The kids wander in packs, stopping occasionally to scream the lyrics to Taylor Swift songs together. There's barely any dancing but a lot of horsing around. I wander around saying, "Put Riley down! You can't carry him like that!" or, "Walking feet, walking feet," when they start playing tag. Sometimes I have to break up games where the boys stand in a circle and try to smash each other in the private parts to see who falls to the floor first in the fetal position, but that's as crazy as things get.

And then I spend the rest of the time shouting to the other chaperones over the terrible music while we catch up on life.

At my most recent dance, I watched the school staff handle the kids. I've known these teachers and administrators for years; I've seen how they work. During the day, they keep things organized and calm. Their classrooms run smoothly and they would never dream of letting a hundred kids do a conga line through the hallways. Dances are an entirely different atmosphere than Tuesday mornings during second hour.

While at the dance I could have stood in the hallway and micromanaged all the kids passing me, monitoring their voice levels, their word choices, and how much eyeliner they were wearing. But I didn't do that. It wasn't the time or the place. The teachers could have pulled out math books and science quizzes and taken advantage of some new educational opportunities, but they didn't bother either.

There's a time and a place to be in charge, to make sure things run exactly how you need them to run. And then there are other circumstances when we need to get into the spirit of things and let an event run its course. This is a lesson I've had to learn the hard way, through painful personal experience. But it's also a lesson I've learned plenty well by watching other women struggle—and fail—with their urge to control everything around them.

Here's the truth. Sometimes we're stressed out and it's simply because we're desperate to keep control of something we're not meant
to control. I'd enjoy middle school dances a whole lot more if the kids
came in with books and we read quietly for two hours while Frank
Sinatra was gently piped through the sound system. Perhaps we could
take a break from reading to watch an episode of *Frazier* or *Friends*.
But any fool can see forcing that environment on a pack of tweens is
a recipe for disaster. I'm going to exhaust myself and stress myself out
for no good reason.

The question we've got to ask ourselves is this—am I stressing myself
out because I'm trying to control something that's really not mine to
control? Am I micromanaging what doesn't belong to me?

Excellent management by itself isn't much of a stressor, right? As
long as everything runs smoothly under our watch, our efforts actually
reduce problems. We think ahead, we anticipate every need, and we
have Plan A, B, and C handy in case of a wild card being thrown our
way. It's all fine.

Until it's not all fine. Maybe someone on the committee gets tired
of doing things our way. Maybe a child decides she wants tattoos on
her entire arm. Maybe a cousin stages a coup and reroutes the family
reunion to a date and location we didn't suggest. Then the stress kicks
in. And we start to freak out. Our minds become swirling, whirling
dervishes of agony, anticipating all the wreckage that lies ahead. We
can see the burning pile of former glory that's about to occur—why can't
they? Are they trying to destroy everything?

And now we have made the subtle switch from managing with excellence to being a control freak. It catches even the best of us unaware,
shocking us. We didn't set out to become control freaks. The running
theme in our minds is simply this: this is the way it has to be. It's the
instinctual, unintentional forcing of our own way. No one wakes up in
the morning hoping to be the wicked stepmother. It's just that we know
best and we're not about to let others run this train off the tracks.

These are the sorts of things we find ourselves saying:

"No one understands the real situation here."

"I can't believe they would make that decision."

"Don't they know how long I've been doing this?"

"I can't let them suffer. I need to _____ to fix it."

"Who do they think they are? Who gave them the right to do that?"

Let's pause for a moment while you throw this book across the room because I've hit a nerve. Don't worry; I've hit my own nerve. This is touchy territory, but we need to talk about this before we choke the life out of the people we love and destroy relationships in the process.

There's a critical step in this issue—discernment. We need to be able to discern what areas are under our full control, what areas need to be shared equally among all members of the group, and what areas are clearly none of our business.

Because, obviously, there are some areas where we need to be involved. For example, our home and young families. Our very young children need our presence in their lives in a way they may deeply resent. They hate vegetables, bath time, and going to bed at eight. But this is our territory, ladies. We're called to bust some little chops and teach the short hooligans how to become functioning adults one day. All the work involved in the process can indeed be stressful, but it's a healthy kind of pressure—the sort we can't avoid if we're going to be good parents.

Beyond our parenting, it's obvious our homes, finances, and careers are going to fall into disrepair without our careful attention. This is where we are called to be excellent managers. Our efforts here can't be considered micromanaging.

But then we consider areas where we need to step back and take all the members' opinions into account. For example, let's examine the church, which, by very definition, includes everyone in the congregation. We all have a part to play in the body of Christ, so we need to let everyone play a part. If we really believe what the Bible is saying, God has set the leadership in place to protect and lead us all closer to Christ.

It behooves us to trust their decisions, even if a particular one is not to our liking. And a healthy leadership will be prayerfully considering the needs of the congregation as a whole, not forcing their own will on everyone else. This is how we mutually submit to one another, because Christ submitted for us.

Or, what about our marriages? They're supposed to be made up of two people who stand equal in Christ, with different roles to play. I know the topic of submission isn't fun and has been abusively applied in too many marriages, but we women have some guilt here. Too many of us have been pretending to submit, even convincing ourselves we're submitting, but really we've been quietly manipulating our husbands like they're our children. And it infuriates us when they stand up and refuse to be treated like children anymore. Treating a husband like a full-grown man who can make his own choices is terrifying, I fully admit. But it's also fun and sexy. Tamed men aren't very interesting, I find.

But at least we have some responsibility in our marriage, right? We aren't overlords who can force our husbands to do our bidding, but we have an important role to play. It's okay to manage our part, to communicate our needs, and to work together with our husbands to create a marriage that works well for both parties.

However, there are other situations where we have no business fiddling around. Far too often we're stressed out because we're inserting ourselves into situations where we don't belong at all. Too many of us are trying to circumnavigate others' natural consequences by stepping in and arranging things in a way we find more palatable.

Let me be clear—there are plenty of areas where people are going to make dumb decisions and they are going to suffer the consequences for it. This is the way God set up the world; it's been like this since Adam and Eve started making dumb decisions. Promiscuity leads to unplanned pregnancy and disease. Poor work habits lead to poor grades or a terrible job experience. Crappy financial choices lead to poverty. Driving drunk leads to a jail cell if you're lucky—a grave if you're not. Affairs lead to broken marriages and children who have to split their holidays, birthdays, and other special occasions between different houses.

It's our natural instinct to step in for loved ones and spare them their consequences because when they suffer, we suffer with them. Or, if we can't avoid the consequences, sometimes we accept them on their behalf by raising their children or paying the legal fees or handing them cash whenever they ask.

But too often, if we really look hard, we're sparing *ourselves* the anxiety of watching them suffer. We're sidestepping the difficult conversation where we tell them *no*. We might be preserving the shallow appearance of a good relationship rather than the deeper, rockier experience that may eventually bring about a strong, authentic relationship. Our own anxiety is taking away the consequences God has designed, thus sparing them the lessons they need to learn.

A friend of mine recently told me her brother is about to be homeless. Plenty of her family lives within the area, and they all love him. But they love him enough to let him be homeless for a while. My friend shrugged her shoulders and said, "He's thirty-two! He needs to work more than two days a week at the bowling alley. He's not moving in with us. My parents told him no. He's been going to Mass with Grandma for a few weeks, hoping to win her favor. But she says no too!"

I needed some clarification, so I asked, "Is there a problem? Why does he work only two days a week?"

"He needs to make time for his Whiffle Ball tournaments!" my friend yelled. I didn't even try to stop my hoot of laughter—that guy totally needs to be homeless for a little while. I guess that might just be the cost of being a thirty-two-year-old Whiffle Ball champion.

Like my friend's family, it's time we stop interfering by supplying cash, making excuses, lying for them, or pretending this is just a phase. We feel like we're being kind and loving, but really we're wresting control from God and relying on our own wisdom to solve the problem. It's time to step back and let God take control again.

This feels, quite frankly, *impossible*. A lot of us are still reeling from a few paragraphs ago, where we just learned we're actually microman-agers and control freaks. We had no idea. We thought the problem was everyone else. Accepting that we can do something about our control freak issues, that we can let go of the stress we're causing ourselves, still seems a little far off. How can we possibly stop doing this thing we didn't even realize we were doing? Is it conceivable the solution to this stress lies within us?

No. And yes. I think the decision to stop micromanaging starts with our own will, but the power to do it only comes from the Holy Spirit who lives within us. It starts by recognizing we can only be responsible for ourselves and the limited territory God has given us. We also rec-ognize that our motives can run amok and become self-serving without even realizing it. We need to turn to the Holy Spirit for wisdom and discernment when the boundaries are smudgy and we can't see clearly.

> The decision to stop micromanaging starts with our own will, but the power to do it only comes from the Holy Spirit.

This passage from James 3:13–18 gives us a place to start. This is what we're looking for:

If you are wise and understand God's ways, prove it by living an honorable life, doing good works with the humility that comes from wisdom. But if you are bitterly jealous and there is selfish ambition in your heart, don't cover up the truth with boasting and lying. For jealousy and selfishness are not God's kind of wisdom. Such things are earthly, unspiritual, and demonic. For wherever there is jealousy and selfish ambition, there you will find disorder and evil of every kind.

But the wisdom from above is first of all pure. It is also peace loving, gentle at all times, and willing to yield to others. It is full of mercy and the fruit of good deeds. It shows no favoritism and is always sincere. And those who are peacemakers will plant seeds of peace and reap a harvest of righteousness.

Notice that we don't get to bail out or abandon the situation. This passage from James still indicates we're to be intimately involved in our family and community. We're called to do good things, but to do them with the right motives—wise, humble, and pure motives. Hiding our selfish ambitions doesn't lead to the kind of fruit that the Holy Spirit wants to grow in our hearts; the selfish ambitions lurking beneath will inevitably surface and always lead to disorder and evil of every kind. The situation will get worse, not better, when we're micromanaging instead of wisely interacting. Our stress levels will go higher when we're trying to control outcomes that aren't ours to control.

Psalm 46:10 is a verse we reference pretty frequently. It states, "Be still, and know that I am God! I will be honored by every nation. I will be honored throughout the world." But did you know "be still" translates these other ways: to let loose, let go, hang limp, weaken, sink, and fail? If we reread that verse with those other definitions, we get a new understanding of the verse. We're actually encouraged to let loose of the problem. Even failure isn't really an issue if it leads to God's power working through the situation. Lowering our stress requires letting go of what we're not meant to grip. We need to release our grasp, and seek God's direction instead of relying on our own. Seeking this will lead us to one place—the humility Christ showed. Humbly resting in God's all-powerful response to our situation is the most peaceful place to be.

We'll never have to freak out when someone stages a coup again. Fine. Let them plan the reunion. Let the child tattoo her entire torso. The church will be fine with the new approach to women's ministry—it might even grow! We'll sit back, pray over the situation, and let God control the outcome.

And yes, sometimes it will all go terribly wrong. There will be times our loved ones end up without rent money or with impossible credit card bills. The church might indeed fall apart or the husband may come home with a BMW with leather seats and twenty-inch rims. But we can choose to let God be God, and then relax into his provision and care. We can respond with wisdom and humility.

(Although it's entirely possible the husband may be sleeping in that BMW for the foreseeable future. We're never going to be saints.)

Make It Personal

1. What is stressing you out because it's not responding to your plan or efforts? Is this an area that's in or out of your God-given territory?
2. What is the very worst thing that could happen if you stopped trying to force the outcome you wanted? Could this actually be God's allowed consequence or plan?

Scripture Focus

"Come, see the glorious works of the LORD: See how he brings destruction upon the world. He causes wars to end throughout the earth. He breaks the bow and snaps the spear; he burns the shields with fire. 'Be still, and know that I am God! I will be honored by every nation. I will be honored throughout the world'" (Ps. 46:8–10).

A Prayer for Today

Heavenly Father, I have no idea of how to release control of areas I'm not intended to control. And many times I can't tell what is mine to manage, what belongs to all of us, and what belongs to you. Please give me humility and pure motives, and please help me to rest in the consequences even when I don't like them. Amen.

Why We Love Our Plump, Forgetful, Messy Friends the Most

On Perfection

A FEW YEARS ago, we saved all our pennies and took the kids to Disney World. Eric and I expected this to be the most sacrificial vacation in the history of Clemence family vacations, because it's ridiculous for adults to spend so much money to see a fake castle and fake princesses. But it turned out pretty swell. We loved the parks, and I drink out of a Miss Piggy coffee mug most mornings, wishing I was still there. Disney works hard to project an image of perfection for each and every guest. Every attraction, view, and ride is carefully designed to help visitors feel like they're actually in the jungle, a fantasyland, or Hollywood.

Let's take a moment to discuss the princesses. I had so many questions. I wanted to know where they find the girls who look like the classic cartoons. How do they train them to act like that? Who makes their dresses? How do they stay in character through all those cute little girls and groaning little brothers? How can you be that patient for that long? That's what I want to know.

I don't know how they do it, but somehow those princesses project an image for all those little girls that is completely consistent with what they've come to know and love on the big screen. They've managed perfection in human form, if only for a few hours a day. They get to wear a beautiful ball gown and a wig and smile and wave at children all day—wait a minute, that sounds really hard. Pretending to be a pretty, pretty princess cannot be an easy job, especially when you add in the Orlando heat. Those ladies must be ninja-level perfectionists.

I have a friend from way, way back who had this perfectionistic impulse to a shocking degree, and I don't think she even recognized it. (She was not actually a princess, Disney or otherwise.) After a while it became difficult to even be with her, because her judgmental radar was always humming. She wasn't malicious about it, just relentless. There seemed to be a deep, underlying need for her to prove her perfection to anyone in the vicinity. If a small problem or failure popped up, she'd throw any person, anywhere, under the bus to distance herself from the issue. She also made sure to point out all mistakes anyone else made. It would have been funny if it hadn't been so dang annoying. I got sick of being called out for weird little things normal people wouldn't even have mentioned, and I also got sick of the Let's Adore Sally and Talk About How Perfect She Is Game.

I honestly don't think she meant to do this. She just couldn't help it. There was a drive deep inside to be perfect in every way, and somehow she needed everyone to see that perfection. She never appeared to notice that it drove a wedge between her and her friends. Eventually we all stopped trying because she was just too exhausting.

It would have been a lot better for everyone if she'd just relaxed, decided being perfect was stupid, and had given herself permission to have normal standards. Get plump, get fired, get wrinkly. Those are the things our friends find comforting and endearing, not a spectacular career, the nicest clothes, or a perfect family smiling with big toothy grins at the camera.

Sure, imperfection makes us vulnerable and open to criticism, but it also builds bridges and makes us accessible. In Jen Hatmaker's *For the Love*, in the chapter titled "Porches as Altars," Jen talks about the beautiful, Christ-honoring community that develops when we prioritize deep relationships. Her edict? Invite people over and feed them, and the lower the standards, the better. Simple. She follows with this word:

> My best advice is just to show up and be truthful. Be the kind of friend you are hoping for. Trust me, no one wants a perfect friend who can't offer a minute of transparency. We can get that on Pinterest. Our souls ache for real people in real homes with real kids and real lives. We may carefully curate online identities with well-chosen pictures and selective information, but doing so leaves us starving for something true. I seek only friends who bleed and sweat and laugh and cry. Don't fear your humanity; it is your best offering.[8]

We tend to cover up our sweat and humanity for our carefully filtered social media posts. Of course, we can be happy about our blessings and then share our joy, but too often our motives are hidden, even to ourselves. Do we recognize our boasting as actual boasting? I doubt it; it's natural to be blind to our own dumbness. We're not consciously trying to one-up our friends, but we do have a desire to be respected in our social circles. We can engage in a silent comparison war without even the first clue we've picked up a weapon and we're about to decimate our friends.

Humans can be kind of terrifying like that, and this isn't a modern problem. Way, way back in the olden days, back when Paul's scribe was writing with a quill and bottle of squid ink (my actual historical knowledge of ancient writing implements is sketchy, so let's not get caught up in the details), he was battling this same issue. Well, his issue was a little bit more sanctified, because a few leaders in the early church were squabbling about who had more authority over the believers. So they were having a churchy fight, not a social media competition.

But we understand his situation when he writes, "Oh, don't worry; we wouldn't dare say that we are as wonderful as these other men who tell you how important they are! But they are only comparing themselves with each other, using themselves as the standard of measurement. How ignorant!" (2 Cor. 10:12).

These men were having a little competition to see who was better, but instead of using an actual, objective measurement, they were reducing everything to subjective opinions. They'd ditched God's standards and Christ's example. We do exactly the same thing. We get caught up in education and success, careers and ministry, numbers and stats and square footage of houses, and completely leave our dear Jesus in the dust.

No wonder we're stressed out—our goals are completely catawampus. If you'll remember, Jesus had simple, objective standards. Love God; love others. That's what we're supposed to focus on, and anything else just causes us more stress. You know what strikes me about this? The absolute freedom we have within those two criteria. Do you know how many ways there are to love God? Be a minister, a singer, a missionary, a parent, a goofball writer, a chef—it really doesn't matter. Just dig deeply into your soul, orient it right to Jesus, and go live the life you have. Whatever he's given you to work with, use it.

> Jesus had simple, objective standards. Love God; love others.

There are just as many ways to love others. We don't all have to serve in the nursery and sing in the choir. Teach, hug, invite for dinner, lose at Monopoly, bake pies, fix the car, run a company, vacuum the carpet, or scrub a poopy butt for the tenth time this morning.

I, the worst mother of tiny children in God's great world, don't have to feel guilty for not having ten babies and then adopting twenty more. I get to take care of three people in my house and then love all of you by writing these words. You, the engineer with the mediocre social skills, can love others by quietly analyzing the moving truck and efficiently packing everything inside as the pastor's family moves to a new house.

I don't have to prove my perfection when I'm just doing my thing, constantly orienting myself to the idea of loving God and loving others.

You don't either. You do you, sister. Maybe your kitchen is a disaster and you haven't cleaned the toilets since you moved in three years ago. Doesn't matter. Ignore the idiot on Instagram who posted her glorious, gourmet kitchen with the shiny granite countertops. Maybe you're too busy holding your sick baby or showing up at the nursing home three days a week. You do you.

The more we welcome our strengths and stop freaking out over our weaknesses, the stronger our bond grows with the people around us. Authenticity breeds freedom, grace, and joy. Relief. We know God works through weakness, anyway. The apostle Paul said he'd rather boast about his weak spots. That's when he most keenly felt the power of Christ working (2 Cor. 12:9–10). Paul could have intimidated us all with the amazing visions and ministry God gave him. Imagine if he had lived today and announced all his spectacular accomplishments on his Twitter account. We wouldn't be able to bear it; we'd stop following the arrogant goat in a matter of days. But Paul was ever aware and connected to his weakness, and he knew it developed an entirely new connection with his loved ones. This wasn't a holy competition; it was the power of the Holy Spirit made evident in a life.

There's a powerful difference between those two things, and most of our friends won't even be able to verbalize exactly what it is. But I can guarantee they'll be able to *feel* the difference. When we show up to love them, it will feel remarkably different than when we show up to prove how perfect we are. Connection always feels better and softer than proving we have it all together. It's like how yoga pants feel better than last year's too-tight jeans.

Let's choose the loving, stretchy, forgiving yoga pants and ditch the fake princess ball gown and plastic wig. Life's too short to be stuck up, lonely, and awesome. I think it's far better to be a bit of a mess, totally welcoming, and deeply connected to others than living a fantasy life in a castle in the middle of Florida.

But you can still totally wear that sparkly tiara if you want. You look lovely in it. We'll post selfies on Instagram for everyone to see!

Make It Personal

1. Who always makes you feel terrible because you can never meet their standards? What, specifically, do they do or say?
2. What are two specific ways you can relate more authentically with others? Where do you need to lower standards or be more honest?

Scripture Focus

"This boasting will do no good, but I must go on. I will reluctantly tell about visions and revelations from the Lord. I was caught up to the third heaven fourteen years ago. Whether I was in my body or out of my body, I don't know—only God knows. Yes, only God knows whether I was in my body or outside my body. But I do know that I was caught up to paradise and heard things so astounding that they cannot be expressed in words, things no human is allowed to tell. That experience is worth boasting about, but I'm not going to do it. I will boast only about my weaknesses" (2 Cor. 12:1–5).

For further study, read 2 Corinthians 12:9–10.

A Prayer for Today

Father, I really do want to connect with the people you've given me. I'm tired of the silent (and not-so-silent) standards of perfection. Please help me to be truthful and authentic, even when it makes me vulnerable. May it give others the freedom to be real as well. Help us all to love you and to love each other. Amen.

I Accidentally Just Destroyed Your Day. And Your Oldsmobile.

On Mistakes

MANY, MANY YEARS ago, I was a college student with a terrible summer job, working the night shift in the factory. If you've never been awake at three in the morning in the company of surly men while you move widgets from one box to another box, then you've truly missed out. The summer nights were often blazingly hot and the darkness did little to cool the stifling air, especially on the evenings when I was sent to work between the giant machines that . . . I don't know . . . *made things*, I suppose. I was a little hazy on the details of what exactly we were doing in that factory, because no one bothers to give the college kid a training session on widgets. I just tried to stay awake and keep my fingers out of the gears.

Things were going pretty well the second summer, which would have been between my sophomore and junior years. I'd gotten a better job in a slightly less terrible factory, plus I was working in our local pharmacy on the weekends. My goal was to earn as much money as possible so I could cover my rent for the school year, therefore living with my fun friends instead of my loving but less-fun parents.

One Friday morning I burst into the June sunshine at seven, free for the weekend. It was payday, I had fun things planned, and I would be away from surly coworkers for two entire days. I'd driven my mother's Oldsmobile to work the night before because my car had been acting up, or something. My memory fails on the details, but it doesn't matter because my car isn't the point here. My mom's car is the key vehicle in this story. Mom had just been given this very nice Oldsmobile because her aunt had become too frail to drive, and we all loved it. It had leather seats, fancy thermostats, and a big, goosey engine. It was far, far nicer than most of the cars our family had ever driven.

(I know you think you know where this is going, but trust me. It's so much worse than what you are picturing.)

So I was driving my mom's precious, new-to-her, free car. I was in a good mood, and I had a lead foot, and I was anxious to get home to get some sleep. The twenty-three miles of secondary roads between Holland and Allegan are a little hilly and curvy, but nothing that an Oldsmobile driven by a nineteen-year-old idiot can't handle.

A garbage truck sedately pulled out in front of me, with plenty of room. I saw him. *I saw the garbage truck, okay?* And I saw the little hill too, but it didn't look too bad. I thought I could definitely see anyone coming over that little blip of a hill ahead. Until I roared the engine, passed the truck, crested the little blip, and *then* saw the oncoming car.

A person has never hit the brakes so hard in her life. I was literally standing on them with my right foot as I swerved back behind the garbage truck and then violently tucked the front end of Mom's Oldsmobile under the truck's bumper.

"Check engine, check engine, check engine," the light blinked at me as I cursed and howled in pain. While I was sitting there, friends from work and school passed me and witnessed the wreckage.

Let's summarize. I've destroyed my mom's car. I'm in terrible, shocking pain. *Then* two cute guys from my graduating class pass me while I'm parked under the garbage truck. Even at that moment I had a pretty good idea I wasn't going to be able to finish out my summer at the factory, which meant I was going to fall short of my financial goals for the summer. If I could have evaporated myself right there, I would have. It was all too much.

As the ambulance pulled up at the hospital, I could hear my frantic mother on the other side of the door. "Is that Jessica in there? Do you have my daughter?" Her poor, sad, weepy voice about killed me, not to mention her exceedingly rare use of my full name. And then, an hour later, after the doctors patched me back up, a police officer came to have a little bedside chat with me. The guy was trying to be awesome, I could tell. He asked if there was any reason I'd smashed into the truck. Maybe a deer had jumped out of a field? The garbage truck didn't give me enough room?

No. I'm just a moron. I confirmed I was totally to blame, so the kind man gave me a ticket right there in the ER and left for other police business.

The rest of the summer was a further lesson in humility. I was capable of destroying a car, my family's finances, my own finances, my health, and my own self-esteem in a two-second decision. This realization came as quite a shock because I'd always considered myself immune to making mistakes that affected other people. I make good decisions, by and large. But this decision landed me in physical therapy for months, I had to quit my job, and my parents had to trade down to a Corsica. A Corsica! Like we were common peasants!

Actually, the Corsica was fine. It was bright blue and lasted for years. But my mom still mourns Aunt Helen's Olds to this day. She makes sad, mewing noises in her throat whenever my siblings bring up my shame.

I guess I should be thankful for the lesson in humility at such a young age. I hate to think of the arrogant woman I might be now, if it weren't for a summer hobbling around and getting gifts like tiny garbage trucks and sweatshirts with garbage trucks printed across the chest.

It was quite the merry gift-giving trend among our friends for a while there. I've almost forgiven them.

If you're in a place where your mistakes have affected other people, I'm completely there with you. I feel your pain, and I might still have the sweatshirt to commemorate the event. We all struggle with our frail humanity, much preferring to believe we're invincible and we don't actually make mistakes. And when we do make those mistakes, we tend to feel like we're the only ones who do that dumb kind of stuff. But no. We're not God. Second Corinthians 4:5–10 reminds us we're human, fragile clay jars, leaking God's light out our human-holes. We contain the great treasure, but we aren't the treasure. And somehow God works through our frailty, proving his greatness through our pitiful, breakable selves.

> We're human, fragile clay jars, leaking God's light out our human-holes.

It's in moments like these that we have to stop the swirling self-accusations and cruel words we lob at our own sweet hearts. We need to remind ourselves that, as Christ-followers, we have two little goals: love God with our heart, soul, and mind, and love others as we love ourselves (Luke 10:27). We're supposed to reflect God's glory to everyone around us, and that can absolutely be accomplished while we're making buffoons of ourselves on a daily basis.

I'm serious. Are you out there loving people and Jesus with each breath? Then don't fret if you hit the garbage truck on Friday morning. Cars can be replaced and new jobs are everywhere.

Did you fail out of school after your parents saved for years to cover your tuition? No problem. You might owe your parents money, but you can live through this. Lots of people fail at school. We don't exile them or anything.

Burned down the house when the grill got out of control? Got fired from your job? Accidentally mowed over your neighbor's prized begonia? It's fine. Life's rough, but we can't let these things destroy our lives. They have nothing to do with our goals of loving God and loving others, and in fact, they may open up new ways to do those things better. I had some intense conversations with God that summer of the garbage truck, as I was stuck at home on painkillers and my friends carried on normal life without me. My relationship with God covered new and important ground with me trapped at home like that.

It's hard to see in the middle of the stress, but these times are often when we see the greatest spiritual growth. When I was humbled that summer, I became a new person. It's never comfortable, but it's rarely a wasted experience. We learn there's no place we can escape from God's love, not even when we embarrass ourselves and make trouble for others. Paul reminds us that "we are pressed on every side by troubles, but we are not crushed. We are perplexed, but not driven to despair. We are hunted down, but never abandoned by God. We get knocked down, but we are not destroyed. Through suffering, our bodies continue to share in the death of Jesus so that the life of Jesus may also be seen in our bodies" (2 Cor. 4:8–10).

Yes. That's what I'm talking about. We're going to disappoint others. It's inevitable. Giving ourselves permission to be human isn't going to change how often we make problems for our loved ones, but maybe it will take some of the sting out of it when we do. Our fragile clay selves are going to get bigger and bigger cracks, but maybe we can let those cracks leak more and more of Jesus's love out to the ones who need it most.

Do you know what's really effective when you're a cracked clay vessel who wants to leak love to others? A sincere apology. I learned this from my dad, and it's a lesson I hope I'll take to my grave. He was always so quick to apologize, and he still is. If he thinks he's offended me, there's an email in my inbox or a call on my phone before I even processed that I might be offended. My father knows he's not perfect, and he manages to love people better because he's fallible. His daughter, who is also quite less than perfect, hopes she follows in his footsteps.

This June marked the twenty-year anniversary of hitting that garbage truck. My mom still misses her car, and my ankle still throbs every day. I still owe that garbage truck driver an apology too. I probably gave him a heart attack. But I also gave him a story to tell for the rest of his life, so that's not too bad. Heaven knows he was only startled up there in the cab, not injured. I barely damaged the garbage truck!

Whatever mistakes you've made, I know you can get through them too. A few decades out, you might have a dull throb and some uncomfortable memories. But these things don't have to drive us to despair or crush us. They just give us further reason to glorify God through our weaknesses.

But, just so you know, passing another vehicle on a hill is highly not recommended by eight out of ten professionals. Even if it's a really little hill and you're absolutely sure no one is coming the opposite way. Feel free to learn from my mistakes—I'm here to serve.

Make It Personal

1. What mistakes do you need to let go of? How will you let them go?
2. Are there things you must say to a loved one to make amends? Anything you need to say to God?

Scripture Focus

"For God, who said, 'Let there be light in the darkness,' has made this light shine in our hearts so we could know the glory of God that is seen in the face of Jesus Christ. We now have this light shining in our hearts, but we ourselves are like fragile clay jars containing this great treasure. This makes it clear that our great power is from God, not from ourselves" (2 Cor. 4:6–7).

A Prayer for Today

Heavenly Father, thank you for loving me even when I goof it all up. My intentions are good, but my ability to complete them perfectly is pitiful. Please help me see when my mistakes affect those around me, and help me make amends where possible. May I continually reflect your love and glory, no matter what kind of mess I've gotten myself into. Amen.

Yes, I Can Do Three Hundred Things on Tuesday

On Overscheduling

OUR FRIENDS FROM Great Britain sent us a calendar for Christmas. It came in a little surprise package, right before the holidays, and I nearly died of happiness to find it on my doorstep. With the calendar, Joseph also included a book he wanted me to read and some propaganda about visiting their little corner of England. The calendar is full of beautiful pictures of the Herefordshire area, so I joyfully hung it on the nail next to the fridge.

Except there's one little problem. No, two. First of all, it has all the British holidays noted, which is kind of weird. They have no need to announce the Fourth of July or Thanksgiving, but they did put in a few random bank holidays. I've been celebrating British banking holidays all year with cake in addition to all the normal American things we celebrate with cake, which means I now weigh fifteen stones. I need to lay off the cake.

The other problem is that it has all the days listed in a vertical format, and each day gets a two-inch line. Either Europeans have very light scheduling needs, or this particular calendar designer was trying to save paper. All year long I've been trying to mash all our family appointments onto those tiny lines, and I've had to revert to code. SM means small group. YG means youth group. There are a few others, but I can't remember what they are, and I probably need to apologize to some people for missing a bunch of things.

There are Sunday nights where I lie in bed and dread the upcoming week because all my little calendar lines are full to the brim. I can feel all the days and the things breathing down my neck. I get up and make a nice long list to calm my anxiety, and sometimes that list is broken down into tiny boxes from 6:30 a.m. to 9:00 p.m. The list helps, because then at least I know I won't forget something. But the list also points out that I have a really big problem. I have totally failed at my efforts to control our schedule. I can't keep up this pace for long.

I bet you can't either. Good Christians know that in times like this we retreat behind Jesus's words in Matthew 11:28. "Come to me, all of you who are weary and carry heavy burdens, and I will give you rest," he said. We have this painted on our walls and imprinted on our coffee mugs, like the phrase itself is some sort of magic talisman that will fix our problems. We want the idea to become the reality with wishes and fairy dust.

Have you ever noticed how that never actually works? While I absolutely do experience Christ's peace in the middle of my chaotic schedule when I take the time to pray, this usually only works for a few moments. The appointments and carpool and jobs are waiting with bated breath for me to utter my "amen" and get back to business. When Jesus said, "Come to me," could he have meant something different than a quick smack of divine energy?

In that passage in Matthew, Jesus continued on and said, "Take my yoke upon you. Let me teach you, because I am humble and gentle at heart, and you will find rest for your souls. For my yoke is easy to bear, and the burden I give you is light" (Matt. 11:29–30). Jesus wants to teach us, which goes further than that quick smack of divine energy. His gentle, humble heart will give us rest for our souls, but only if we're actually changing because of what we're learning from him.

Our cluttered calendars and overloaded schedules are evidence of what is important to us. I think it's possible that instead of learning from Jesus and choosing his yoke, we're doing whatever we want and sprinkling a little Jesus over the top of it. We've turned him into holy sprinkles to make our daily choices palatable, but what we need is a completely new approach.

> Cluttered calendars and overloaded schedules are evidence of what is important to us.

Let's give ourselves permission to imagine living with a totally new approach to time management. Let's mentally clear our calendars and start with nothing but time and space. What would it look like if we only added things that could be seen as evidence of following Jesus? We'd need time for loving God and loving others, which would require a nice block for meeting together with other believers in corporate worship, but also in small, more casual groups. "Small groups" is what we call them at our church. Your church probably has some trendy new name for a group of people who get together and eat a lot and study the Bible as they get to know each other intimately during the week.

I see a clear benefit for children's and youth programming, in part because my own daughter flourishes in a youth group setting. I love that she has a place to learn about God and make safe friendships. It makes a huge difference for her, and I know that youth groups are the only safe places some kids have in this crazy world. We'd be silly to cut them off from that love and biblical teaching. And this is going to ruffle some feathers, but I think that's it for church programming. The end. I'd far rather see a congregation fully participating in a few genuinely helpful activities than a hundred shallow ones.

I think we take all the church activities too far. We're programming ourselves to death, but not really seeing a benefit in our spiritual lives or in the lives of the unchurched. The early church met together for worship and teaching, ate together, shared Communion, and tried to survive the hungry lions together. They did not have time to fiddle with

VBS and five different Bible studies and group trips and weekend-long women's retreats and a monthly men's breakfast.

I'm not saying any of those things are *wrong*, I'm just saying that it's possible to load up a calendar with a lot of religious things but never actually get close to Jesus in the midst of it all. And in the middle of all the meetings, are we really getting a chance to know the people next to us? Is there room for authentic relationships to grow in a budget meeting?

There ends my diatribe on church calendars, but we still need to address the one that hangs next to our fridge at home. Now that we've made time for loving God corporately, we must make time for growing in a personal relationship with him. We need to add a daily time of Bible reading and prayer. So often our crowded calendars leave no time for reading the Word or listening to the Holy Spirit. For years I thought I could skip this step. I thought parking my body in a pew for an hour on Sundays and engaging in other (aforementioned) activities meant God and I were set. When I finally started to read the Bible and pray on a daily basis, the change in my heart and worldview was shocking. I'd been so close to the truth, but so far away.

After we tend to our own spirits, we move to our families. We probably have jobs. We might have small children who need constant care or elderly relatives who need ongoing assistance. The physical home has to be attended to, and heaven knows someone needs to get the groceries.

Some of us are in a season where there's literally no time left after caring for our families and making God a priority. That's it. We're done. But those seasons end eventually, and we're left with some flexible time. That's when we can fit in all the meetings and civic programs and who knows what else is on your calendar right now.

What would change in our lives if we actually reworked our entire calendar and acknowledged our true priorities? How far off is this ideal from our daily lives?

I know some of you are right on track. You may need to make some tweaks here and there, but by and large your priorities line up with your beliefs, and your energy and time are all going to the best places possible. Good for you! You might be really tired, but I bet you're tired in the very best way possible.

However, some may be quietly realizing that your priorities are clear on the calendar, just as it stands, and you like it this way. Just imagining your life without all the activities makes you a little anxious. You might be realizing your children's sports schedules are more important than church and you can't imagine giving them up to sit in a pew every week. Or, you might be seeing that you'd far rather go to ten church meetings than make time to get to know an unbeliever out in the real world. You'd rather watch a Netflix marathon than pick up your Bible.

I totally understand. I've had such realizations over the years. But whether we like it or not, our calendars point to the truth. Just like our bank statements are evidence of our financial priorities, our calendars show what we do with our time. It's hard to absorb the truth, but it may be the most important thing we ever struggle to accept. But once we accept it, we can do something about it. We can fix this! We don't have to live stressed-out lives with a thousand things crammed into every day. We can choose our priorities and then live them.

As the year has meandered on, I've gotten used to those little lines on our British calendar. I'm happy to note there are even blocks of time with nothing written on them. I've been spending more time hanging out with the family and less time running all over the county for less important things. Our friends are on the calendar for Friday night, because that's important. Helping at a carnival and then attending an anniversary party have made it onto Saturday's line, because those are two ways we care for our community and our extended family. Those have made the cut.

Last night we realized we had a free evening, and we took the kids to a special showing of *Twister*. Eric and I saw that movie on our first date, just before I hit the garbage truck (please see the previous chapter if you're bouncing around through the book). The screening included theater employees throwing Styrofoam hail at us, inflatable cows swinging through the air from strings, and—heavens, I hope you've seen this movie or you have no idea of what I'm talking about—fans so we could create wind. I don't think the kids will ever forget that spontaneous night, and I'm glad we had the room in our calendar for it.

I know we'll have to keep making room for spontaneous things for years to come. It's easy to fill up all the blocks of time, feeling like we're involved in something important. Sometimes those things are important, but sometimes they just keep us from being where Jesus would have us.

I want nothing more than to be exactly where Jesus is, focused on what he says is important. How about you?

Make It Personal

1. What would your calendar look like if you completely revamped it? How close are you to the ideal?
2. What would happen if you handed Jesus your calendar and told him to make the changes himself? Could you stand to let him have the pen?

Scripture Focus

"Then Jesus said, 'Come to me, all of you who are weary and carry heavy burdens, and I will give you rest. Take my yoke upon you. Let me teach you, because I am humble and gentle at heart, and you will find rest for your souls. For my yoke is easy to bear, and the burden I give you is light'" (Matt. 11:28–30).

A Prayer for Today

Heavenly Father, I'm pretty sure my stress level over the calendar could be fixed by taking your yoke and actually learning from you. Please break through my excuses and preferences to show me what's really important. Please don't let religious busyness and the expectations of others keep me from you. Amen.

Well, Someone Has to Be Fodder for the Evening News

On Restoration After a Sin

Do you ever watch the news and wonder about the rest of the story? What happens to those people once the scandal is over? I never used to care much until a few years ago, when two completely unrelated news stories hit pretty close to home. Suddenly the concept of terrible choices and consequences didn't seem so vague and impersonal. My usual attitude of "Good, serves them right," didn't cover people I actually knew. It only worked for strangers who had done bad things and then deserved bad consequences.

I've learned a lot the last few years, thankfully. I'm much less quick to judge and heap coals on heads, and I have those very painful and stressful situations to thank for that. Learning mercy is painful and stressful, but gives life in the end.

Once a sin is committed and found out, it's hard to piece a life back together. What does a person do after such a destructive choice? How do we recover and move on once we've devastated our own lives? The wreckage can seem too much to even sort through; the pieces too far flung to mend back together. And yet, we must. We don't keep a hinterland full of ex-cons, ex-adulterers, or ex-thieves—they're all here right among us, trying to rebuild. Australia isn't entirely populated with criminals anymore. Right?

Could I be talking to you? I don't ask because I'm pointing fingers; I ask because I see you over there, and I don't want you hanging your head in shame one minute longer. I have some things to say and I hope you'll find them encouraging.

I see that you understand the enormity of the sin, you've repented, and you've made amends. You aren't hiding and pretending it will all go away if you close your eyes and wish hard enough. Things are way past hiding and wishing.

Whatever the situation, the worst has happened. The sin was committed and discovered, and now you're living in what was probably your worst nightmare for a while—this messed-up, broken-up life is what you were trying to avoid. That's the bad news. The good news is that I'm sitting right here in the middle of it with you, and so are a lot of your friends and family.

We're here to show you grace and mercy, even when you doubt our sincerity. We want you whole again. We really do. We're so very aware of our own sins and failings, and this makes us kind and gentle. You may not understand the depth of our love for you. Trust us, it's deep. At any moment, any of us could walk the same path—or even a far worse one—so please believe that we're not here on a witch hunt. This is a gathering of mercy.

Our Father has extended his unending mercy to you; please let us do the same. And, may I suggest you extend some mercy to yourself? I know you might feel like branding your forehead with your sin or sewing your scarlet A to the front of your blouse, but let's not. Honestly, if God was into branding us with our sins, who among us would have enough skin for the marks? We'd be tattooed with our shame from head to foot. He doesn't do that, and we shouldn't do it to ourselves.

Let's walk forward together, arm in arm, with our heads held high. There is no condemnation for those of us in Christ Jesus, we read in Romans 8:1–2. Because we belong to him, the Spirit has freed us. Sin can no longer drag us to our deaths, so let's tell the shame to back off and give us some breathing space. While we breathe in the mercy, let's start rebuilding a new life, okay? Let's give the Holy Spirit control of our minds and lead us to life and peace (Rom. 8:6).

On the days when the shame comes rushing back in and you lose the will to fight the same old battle again, please don't give up. Fight. Fight for us. For our sakes, please keep going. Keep living and breathing and trying. We need to see your redemption story. We need to know that when we fail—which is a certainty—his mercy will cover us too.

Is his grace really sufficient? We're watching you to see.

We need to see your life on the other side of failure, and we need to know restoration is possible. Please, let us watch you start fresh. Let us see you reach out to your community and church with new love, even when that love is scarred and not as shiny as it used to be. Our love isn't always shiny either, but we still need to know we can offer it.

Please hear me. Rebuilding your family, life, and ministry may be the most courageous and generous thing you ever do.

Do you know how close we all are to being on the news ourselves? My brother-in-law is an attorney, and he's fond of saying that we're all just one bad decision away from jail. All of us. He's not wrong, sister. We're all one tantrum, greedy thought, or lustful decision away from a terrible mug shot on the Channel 8 news. We need to know that no matter what happens, we have hope.

> We're all just one bad decision away from jail. All of us.

Some of us haven't committed one enormous, destructive sin, but we still carry the weight of our daily transgressions. We're burdened by the secrets we hide, hoping no one will see. It could be a habit of lying or a friendship bordering on an emotional affair. Perhaps our lack of discipline has led to overspending or overeating that's causing us deep shame. God's grace is sufficient for us too. The same process of repentance, seeking God's presence, and starting over lead us back to wholeness and health.

And now I speak to the rest of us, gathered around our friend and sister. We're all here together, watching someone start fresh. How can we come alongside her and make her restoration easier? What can we offer? Let's start with a normal conversation, normal contact, normal everything. Keep texting her silly things. Tell her those pants make her butt look huge. Make her pluck her eyebrows. Bring her coffee and, moment by moment, drag her back into the light of day. Don't treat her like she's contagious or somehow too fragile to go into public. No, I say. Take her to the beach and the mall and the tourist trap. Take her to Costco and make her carry your enormous package of toilet paper from way in the back of the store.

Whatever it takes to help her feel normal and forgiven and fresh, you do that. Remind her of the future, and then hand her another package of toilet paper to keep her mind off her troubles.

And let's go further. Let's intentionally seek others who are rebuilding. Hire the convict. Invite the adulterer. Include the drug addict and the embezzler.

No. Let me rephrase that. Hire your brother. Invite your sister. Include everyone, without regard for past sins. This is too important to get wrong. Romans says this:

> We are made right with God by placing our faith in Jesus Christ. And this is true for everyone who believes, no matter who we are. For everyone has sinned; we all fall short of God's glorious standard. Yet God, in his grace, freely makes us right in his sight. He did this through Christ Jesus when he freed us from the penalty for our sins. For God presented Jesus as the sacrifice for sin. People are made right with God when they believe that Jesus sacrificed his life, shedding his blood. . . . God did this to demonstrate his righteousness, for he himself is fair and just, and he makes sinners right in his sight when they believe in Jesus. (Rom. 3:22–26)

Jesus. It's all about what Jesus did to bring us into a right relationship with the Father, and—heaven help us—each other. The reason we're so ashamed of our behavior is that it's shameful. It truly is. But that shame needs to be replaced with joy and righteousness when we realize that Christ has made us right with God.

How can we deny Christ's sacrifice by continuing to carry our shame? How can we continually remind our sister of her failure when Jesus's blood has covered it?

If we truly believe what we read in the Bible, we can't. We either believe it or we don't. Sure, some days we might wrestle the shame to the ground and come up bloody and exhausted, but we keep going. We keep accepting our status as beloved, forgiven daughters. We keep loving, reaching out, and starting over.

I don't watch the news much anymore. The weight of all those souls is too much for me to bear. I worry about their mothers and their families; I worry about their jobs and their futures. But I have learned how to love once the worst is over and it's time to rebuild. And knowing how to help a person start over takes away a lot of the stress, honestly. The worst can happen and we can all survive it. We can even come out stronger, more loving, and gentler.

You might need this exact message today, right where you are. Or maybe a friend needs it. Maybe Future You and Me need it. When the time comes, may there be mercy. Because we have been shown mercy, may we stop at nothing until we show it to others.

Make It Personal

1. Who among you needs a new start? What can you do to help her feel normal and forgiven and fresh?
2. Are you in need of mercy? Do you believe God can truly restore you?

Scripture Focus

"Have mercy on me, O God, because of your unfailing love. Because of your great compassion, blot out the stain of my sins. Wash me clean from my guilt. Purify me from my sin. For I recognize my rebellion; it haunts me day and night. . . . Create in me a clean heart, O God. Renew a loyal spirit within me. Do not banish me from your presence, and don't take your Holy Spirit from me. Restore to me the joy of your salvation, and make me willing to obey you" (Ps. 51:1–3, 10–12).

A Prayer for Today

Heavenly Father, there are some sins so devastating we don't know if recovery and restoration are possible. They seem so deep and dark that we fear your light can never penetrate them. Help us to see differently, Father. Pierce our darkness with your light. May we always remember Christ's sacrifice and that it covers our sin. Help us to show ourselves mercy, and may we reach out to our sisters who need a fresh start. Amen.

My White-Hot Hate for the Carpet

On Discontentment

My white-hot, burning hate is currently aimed at the carpet in our house. We had this home built about four years ago, and I already detest the carpet. This is the very definition of a first-world problem, I understand, but here's the thing. When we sat down with the building team, we had a very specific budget in mind. We chose not to upgrade certain items because we didn't want to amortize interest for thirty years on things we could easily upgrade ourselves (with cash) at a later date. What we didn't count on was that while the carpet looked lovely at installation, it's basically apartment-grade flooring. It's the exact stuff you'd purchase if you were a landlord and a crew of fraternity brothers had signed a lease. You're going to be keeping their damage deposit because they're absolutely about to do unspeakable things to that rug.

What's cheap? The cheapest of the cheap? That's what you'd buy, and that's what we have in our house. Luckily, we're not a crew of frat brothers, so the carpet held up pretty well for a few years. But now the constant wear has rubbed tracks where the carpet fibers are breaking down. I'm sitting here right now, darting looks at it between typing words, and it's taking all my physical restraint not to get up and rip it out with my fingernails. We won't even go into what the cat has done to the flooring on the lower level of the house, because I believe we've already covered that at length. Let's just say that one of these days I'm going to be in Sackett's Flooring Solutions with the credit card, and Eric had better be there to stop me.

This is one of the advantages of being forty years old. *Now* I understand that buying an entire house of flooring without already having the money in the bank is a terrible, terrible idea. So when Eric tries to stop me, I'll actually let him. I know that my discontentment will launch me into bad decisions that have far worse consequences than just having a few patches of worn carpet. Do you know what's worse than the stress of thwarted desires? The stress of making really stupid decisions that ruin everything later.

That's the thing about discontentment. Giving it room to fester just leads to the dark places of our minds. We lose all reason and sense. We end up buying things without the money, thanks to our modern economic system that lets any fool buy any thing with a swipe of a plastic card.

Or, far worse than a credit card bill is the discontentment that festers, grows, and then leads us away from our commitments, marriages, and vows. It may seem like a small thing to be less than pleased with your husband at the moment, but when it becomes a chronic disappointment that begins to make other men seem more and more appealing, we're looking at a serious problem. When other gentlemen appear more spiritually mature, kind, and successful than our own mates, it takes us directly to all manner of pain.

We know this, don't we? No one thinks outrageous debt or adultery are good ideas—they're universally seen as terrible ways to fix what's really wrong in our lives. But that's what discontentment drives us to; we slowly sink into a world where we become desperate to find joy and fulfillment. Discontentment and the solution to it is not a new problem.

I've made the search for contentment into one of my life projects, because it seems to me that I can avoid some of my greatest stresses by gracefully accepting life's limitations and hardships, and working cheerfully with the resources I've been given. I'm learning that there isn't actually a successful search for contentment, like gold or the Holy Grail—it's a discipline that has to be learned by making one tiny decision at a time. It's a constant acceptance of my circumstances and a constant rejection of selfishness, greed, and American standards.

Sometimes I win; sometimes I lose. These days I'm winning more than losing, which is a comfort. Peace is so often a hard-chosen state of mind and not an endless succession of happy days. I didn't understand this for a long time, which is why Paul's letter to the church in Philippians made no sense to me, no matter how often I read it. He wrote, "Not that I was ever in need, for I have learned how to be content with whatever I have. I know how to live on almost nothing or with everything. I have learned the secret of living in every situation, whether it is with a full stomach or empty, with plenty or little. For I can do everything through Christ, who gives me strength" (Phil. 4:11–13).

> Peace is so often a hard-chosen state of mind and not an endless succession of happy days.

Of course Paul could manage this, I thought, because he was some sort of Super Christian. Anyone who could joyfully survive imprisonment, beatings, and shipwrecks for the sake of the gospel clearly wouldn't be pouting about his worn carpet. But Paul said the secret of his contentment was knowing that he could do anything with Christ's strength. Paul didn't get some special, secret strength from Christ. I don't read anywhere in the Bible that some of us can access an entirely new level of the Spirit, like unlocking a level in a video game as we get really good at it. Paul was just completely focused on winning others to Christ, no matter what the cost to him personally. The hard stuff didn't matter because he had a clear goal, and it wasn't room-to-room teak flooring with an ebony stain. It wasn't a knight in shining armor (or a princess in shining armor, in Paul's case) to rescue him from loneliness or even an apartment in a safe and fashionable part of ancient Rome.

Contentment arrives as we willfully choose to be thankful for what we have, use our resources creatively, and willfully refuse to let our desires fester into bad decisions. It's not that we have to be passively content, because many times we can get creative and change things within reason, budget, and life's limitations. Life takes courage too. Sometimes we need to kick things into gear to see how far our creative, courageous spirits can take us.

That blend of courage and contentment requires constant balance. There's often a mingling there, a moment-by-moment weaving together of two very different challenges. For example, let me tell you about this very house with the worn carpet. In the last year, I almost talked my husband into selling it at least three times. Yes, the very house we just built and moved into; that's the thing I wanted to sell. I touched on this situation in an earlier chapter, but there's more to the story than just financial concerns.

This house wasn't quite suiting me, somehow. I couldn't put my finger on it exactly, but it didn't feel like home. I really just felt like I was marking time in someone else's house until I could go and be free and creative in my real house. The thing with living in a new subdivision like this one is that buyers expect a certain level of uniformity when they come to look at it. So, while I might be quite excited to experiment by ripping out the carpet and living with painted subfloors, buyers would not find this charming. They'd probably also reject green kitchen cabinets, a bathroom lined in barn wood, or retro wallpaper in the kitchen. And these are all the exact sorts of design experiments I think are fun.

I was paralyzed from making any inspirational changes because I was afraid of what buyers would think, and since I wanted to sell the house and move right away, I didn't do anything but feel vaguely uncomfortable in my own house.

Eric and I talked it over and prayed about it until the answer became clear. We'd prayed ourselves into this house, and nothing about the situation had changed from a spiritual point of view. Living here, we are still able to travel some and give regularly, and this is exactly where we are supposed to be. I had to find contentment with that realization, and my first step was to break out the paintbrush. The kitchen cabinets had an orange hue I'd tried to ignore (they looked good in the builder's showroom, but I hated the finish when I tried to live with it). I dragged my mom and sister over and drafted them into painting with me. We lost many hours of our lives, but now I have gray cabinets I adore. I found a chandelier at the resale shop for twenty-five dollars and batted my eyelashes at Eric until he installed it for me. I got creative with new cabinet knobs (twenty-five cents for a pack of two!) from the same resale shop, and now I have custom wooden knobs for a few dollars.

I love that room now. It required acceptance and creativity to get there, but the balance finally emerged after fiddling around with it for a while. I obviously can't peer through these pages to see what you're struggling with, but I hope you have a new perspective on your situation. Can you change it? Must you? Then go ahead and forge on in. But if you can't, if you're just stuck for a time, then I hope you have the desire to find a new peace in your circumstances, right where you are.

We all have the same ability to be content in Jesus. It's just a matter of remembering that and having the right focus on what's important, what we can change, and what we need to accept. I'm slowly working on it, and maybe soon I'll be able to title a chapter "My Passionate Adoration for Frayed, Worn, Cheap Carpet."

Make It Personal

1. What is one thing you're desperate to change right now?
2. Is this a situation where you need courage, or acceptance? How will you resolve the issue?

Scripture Focus

"Yet true godliness with contentment is itself great wealth. After all, we brought nothing with us when we came into the world, and we can't take anything with us when we leave it. So if we have enough food and clothing, let us be content" (1 Tim. 6:6–8).

A Prayer for Today

Dear Lord, I know you can see my situation. You know the motivations of my heart, you see the external circumstances, and you know how this all will end. Please help me to have a focus that pleases you. I can't manage this on my own, Father, because I'm desperate to get things fixed down here. Please show me what I need to accept with serenity and please help me to know what requires the courage to change. And please help me learn to cross-stitch so I can get that prayer on my dining room wall. Amen.

A Dumpster and a Bulldozer Would Solve All This

On Clutter and Junk

Spoiler alert: we're about to move to a stressor that's both my pet peeve and my area of expertise.

Spoiler alert number two: I'm not even going to pretend I have any biblical backing for it. So there. I've read a few books where the author veered from absolute scriptural fact to her own opinion and didn't bother to differentiate between the two. A reader without a strong knowledge of the Bible may not be able to disentangle the fact from the opinion, and that grates on me every time. I'm not going to do that to you.

So before we go one step further, let's just accept that this is my own, very strong opinion. You can rip this entire section out of the book and keep on trucking, and God will not smite you with lightning or anything. A few chapters back I talked about seeking peace in our families when their things are making us crazy. That's still good advice—we need to seek peace first. But it's possible the entire family could benefit if we took a look at our stuffed homes and began to dig ourselves out of the mess.

Some of you may be literally suffocating in your own homes right now, as piles and piles of disorganized things creep closer and closer to you. Do you remember that old *Mad TV* sketch, where Michael

MacDonald played a mannequin who slowly inched closer and closer to his victims? They kept looking at him with concern, knowing something was weird, but didn't acknowledge there was a true problem until *he killed them.*

My word, America (and Canada and probably parts of Australia), what is wrong with us? Do you know why I don't have any biblical backing for this chapter? Because this problem didn't even exist back when the ancient scribes were dipping their quills in squid ink! (Yes, we have this historically inaccurate reference once again; I apologize. A little.) Jesus talked a lot about money and possessions and finding our true security as children of God, but he didn't need to address the crowds' stuffed closets and garages and storage units.

Target hadn't been invented yet, so women weren't flocking to the organizational section to buy bins and shelving and decorative baskets to hide their junk.

Honestly, I don't even know if junk had been invented in Jesus's day. Everything just took so darn long to craft by hand. We needed an entire Industrial Revolution, long after Jesus, to mechanize the manufacturing process. One day we had a great idea to make fabric quickly and easily, then BOOM, suddenly every fast food meal for our children comes with a ridiculous toy, packaged in plastic.

Do you ever wonder about the factory workers in China who manufacture all this rubbish for us? Do you ever look through a catalog entirely populated with junk (Oriental Trading, I'm looking at you) and wonder what those poor workers must think of us? I wonder if they even know what those widgets are as they pass by on the assembly line. I hope with all that is within me that they don't think those plastic blinky things are making us any happier.

They're not making us happier, good factory workers of China. They just get lost in weird corners of rooms until eventually we throw them out, adding to the enormous piles in our landfills. And of course we have to fight about landfills all the time, because everyone wants one close and handy but no one wants one in the neighborhood. We want all our plastic-filled, toxin-laden garbage dumps outsourced to a neighborhood we don't frequent.

I long for the days of yore when people owned fewer things, but the things they owned were high quality. Right now I'm sitting in a chair from the 1950s, and I love it with a thousand loves. Thanks to my great-aunt's piles of money, much of the furniture she bought back in the day is still being used on a daily basis. Yes, the upholstery is getting worn, but my word—it's sixty years old! My husband's grandparents owned a china cabinet that's now in our kitchen, holding all our Fiesta dinnerware. The frame is solid and the drawers still slide in and out with ease. Bless it.

We've substituted cheap, fast, and vast for quality and common sense. Not that this is doing us a lick of good, by the way. We can't find anything. Do we own it? Yes, of course. Can we locate it? Probably not. Whatever it is, it's probably buried under a load of other things we can't remember buying or needing. Why do we put up with this stress?

I don't think we should. I'm not even going to advocate that you try to organize your stuff; I'm going to try to convince you to get rid of most of it. And further, I'm going to attempt to convince you to stop bringing it into the house in the first place.

Here, let me tell you a few stories to motivate you. In their book *Everything That Remains*, friends Ryan and Joshua decided to become minimalists together. Both of them had high-pressure jobs for a technology corporation, and one day Joshua woke up and realized he had no idea why he needed a huge condo and all those clothes when he was only one person. It's not like he could wear three suits at a time. Downsizing commenced. Little by little, he dug his way out of debt, out of owning a suffocating amount of things, and into freedom. He convinced his best friend Ryan to join in, but Ryan was a little more hesitant. He couldn't quite convince himself to give up all his things cold turkey, so the two of them took a weekend and boxed up everything in Ryan's house.

And I mean *everything*. They literally put everything but the cat into boxes, then left them right in Ryan's three-bedroom home. As Ryan needed something, he unpacked it. That was the rule. If he didn't actually need it, it stayed in the box. By about the tenth day of the experiment, he had stopped unpacking boxes. He realized that everything he needed was pretty much a tiny fraction of what he owned. He started to rethink his car payment, his eleven-hour work days to pay for his fancy car and his huge condo, and his electronic gizmos. He started to rethink why he bought and did everything.

Within months Joshua and Ryan had jettisoned all that held them back, including their taxing jobs, and started an entirely different kind of life. This isn't just possible for two single men in Ohio. It's possible for me, and it's possible for you too.

I have already admitted that I stand in my closets frequently and evaluate the contents, but I also do it in the basement utility room, the garage, and my kitchen. I say this not so you can crown me with adoration but because I can't understate the relief this has been. Do you know how wonderful it feels to not have piles of unused things taking up your breathing room? It feels like heaven. I would love for you to get rid of the clutter and stress and trade it for something much, much lighter.

> Do you know how wonderful it feels to not have piles of unused things taking up your breathing room? It feels like heaven.

Last week we helped our friends move into a new apartment. I stood in the tiny apartment kitchen, looked around, and realized I could make that space work with my own cooking things if I needed to. Fifteen years ago, I would have thought I was nuts. But now I've culled all of our kitchen stuff down to only the things we use all the time. We do have a few specialty baking pans that might not make the cut if we actually moved to a house with a tiny kitchen, but those things could be gathered in less than five minutes and put in a small box.

The waffle iron still grieves me, though. We use it so infrequently that it probably should go, but there are times when only a waffle will suffice on a cold Saturday morning. That thing is on the fence. I have my eye on you, Mr. Waffle Maker That Takes Up Space but Also Provides Delicious Waffles.

Not convinced? Joshua Becker, Tsh Oxenreider, Marie Kondo, and Dee Williams all agree with me. (Go ahead, look them up. Consider it homework with immediate rewards.) There are all kinds of people across the modern world who are buying tiny houses, living out of a backpack, or culling their possessions down to the bare minimum. Some of them have only thirty-three items in their wardrobe and wear only their favorite, best pieces. Some of them experiment with living with only one hundred objects, or traveling around the world out of a suitcase for a year.

Each one has traded a life stuffed to the gills with sadness for freedom and fun. It's like exchanging a snowsuit, woolen hat, huge gloves, and clunky boots for just a pair of shorts and a tank top on a hot day. Relief.

Will people think you're weird? Yes, probably. But now I think people who hoard things are weird, so it's all relative. You can be the weirdo with clean closets and extra money in your bank account, instead of the weirdo who has things land on her head when she opens the cabinet doors. And you can also be the weirdo who doesn't have to work too much or worry about the credit card bill, because you will have found a level of life that is comfortable and affordable.

Good luck, and give me a call if you need help packing up those boxes.

Make It Personal

1. What one room of your home stresses you out the most? What needs to go?

2. Spending-fast challenge: This will help you use up the things you already own in your home and will also create some margin in your finances. Win-win! (If you don't know what I'm talking about, the internet has tons of blogs to help you out.)

Scripture Focus

"I also tried to find meaning by building huge homes for myself and by planting beautiful vineyards. I made gardens and parks, filling them with all kinds of fruit trees. I built reservoirs to collect the water to irrigate my many flourishing groves. I bought slaves, both men and women, and others were born into my household. . . . I had everything a man could desire! . . . But as I looked at everything I had worked so hard to accomplish, it was all so meaningless—like chasing the wind. There was nothing really worthwhile anywhere" (Eccl. 2:4–8, 11).

A Prayer for Today

Dear Lord, I can't believe all this stuff we have. Help me to figure out what we need and use and love, and may the rest be donated to someone else. May my piles of stress be transformed into blessings for the people who need what I don't use. Amen.

So Many Ways This Could All Go Terribly Wrong

On Plans for the future

MY FRIEND MEREDITH and I are kindred souls, of sorts. She and I love to make the wisest possible decisions about the future. We can both nail down an option and then strangle it to death imagining every possible outcome. The bad news is that there's no way to reliably predict the future, so we often drive ourselves mad. The good news is that we've usually thought through most of the possibilities and then chosen well.

So, basically, we make ourselves crazy, but things turn out okay in the end. There are far worse systems than this, and I think Meredith's going to turn out just fine. She's about fifteen years younger than I am, and just about exactly where I was fifteen years ago—a sweet husband, a cute toddler, and another baby on the way, and they all live in a little tiny starter house that drives her crazy on a daily basis. Her commitment to making good choices is going to serve her well, assuming the stress of making decisions with imperfect data about the future doesn't cripple her (or me) in the process.

That's the thing about decisions, isn't it? It's not that we can't make them; it's that we won't ever have all the information we need. We can plan and plan and plan and then have one incident wipe out years of steady plotting. You get married, start your career, buy your house, and then twins show up in the sonogram. Years later, maybe you finally get those twins off to college and one of them returns with your unplanned grandchild. Or maybe you've been saving for retirement for decades, and just before you clear out the office and leave for Spain, your spouse has a heart attack and needs six months of rehab.

There's just no telling what will happen. This is, of course, infuriating. I'd be so much less stressed out if I had all the information I need.

> There's just no telling what will happen. This is, of course, infuriating.

I'm not sure why God insists on giving us a partial view of the future without a smidgen of the nitty-gritty details. Even Jesus's disciples struggled with this in Matthew 24. That chapter contains some of the most jaw-dropping, terrifying things we have on record from Jesus's mouth. The disciples had pointed out the temple buildings, and Jesus retorted with, "Do you see all these buildings? I tell you the truth, they will be completely demolished. Not one stone will be left on top of another!" (v. 2).

The men were understandably concerned. If something was about to happen to the temple, to the very center of their religious structure, they wanted to know when and how and what the results were going to be. So they asked Jesus when it was going to happen and what signs would signify the time had approached.

That's when Jesus launched into the truly terrifying stuff, telling them about wars, threats, famines, and earthquakes. He followed with warnings of persecution, deception, and fleeing through the hills. "How terrible it will be for pregnant women and for nursing mothers in those days," he said (v. 19). That verse scared me to death for years. When Caleb was in preschool I finally relaxed, knowing we could flee a little more easily. (Also, I started some anti-anxiety medication not long after that, which helped as well. I do not claim to be the most emotionally stable woman in the world.)

Jesus continued to list unsettling things that would signify his return, the moment his followers have been straining to see for two thousand years. He promised we'll see him on clouds of glory, and there will be a great blast of the trumpet. His angels will gather his chosen ones from the ends of the earth, and that's when we'll finally be home where we belong.

However, as if we didn't have enough mystery to sort through, he then said, "However, no one knows the day or hour when these things will happen, not even the angels in heaven or the Son himself. Only the Father knows" (v. 36).

How on earth are we supposed to function with this limited information? If only the Father knows exactly the time, that means everyone else on the face of the planet—and a lot of beings above the face of the planet—are all just waiting for the signal.

> How on earth are we supposed to function with this limited information?

When I was a kid, every time I lost my parents in a public place, I assumed the rapture had happened without me. I figured I'd somehow missed out on the key ingredient of salvation and the angels had left me to my own devices. I still worry about that sometimes, but now I focus on that trumpet blast Jesus promised us. If I haven't heard the trumpet, it just means my family is wandering loose somewhere in the building and I need to start texting until one of them feels a phone vibrate in a butt pocket.

Again, I have digressed. I apologize. Jesus acknowledged that we wouldn't know when it is going to happen, so we need to live faithful lives of anticipation. It's like a servant who knows her master will be back at some point, and she doesn't want to be caught sleeping on the job. (Or surfing the internet on company time, more likely.) She does her best, knowing at any moment the boss could throw open the door. She doesn't want to be humiliated when he does. We want our decisions to indicate that we're absolutely ready for his examining eyes. No one wants to disappoint the Lord when he suddenly appears.

However, in light of eternity, I don't think our small decisions really matter all that much. We might be obsessing over what house to buy, when to get married, how many kids to have, or whether we can afford the newer car. We might be making ourselves completely crazy because these things mean a lot to us right now, but eternally speaking, they're very inconsequential. Everything we see and feel will be washed away as God sets up his eternal kingdom.

What does matter is that we're faithful in what we can see and understand right now. What house we buy won't matter nearly as much as whether we choose to honor God and care for those around us. God will honor faithful, worshipful decisions. He will be with us when things happen that are completely out of our control. We're adults; we understand that the worst can happen. Cancer happens. Job losses happen. We fear what we can control and we fear what we can't control, but our future is held in the hands of an all-knowing, all-prepared God. He is able to keep us steady. There's no decision that is out of his hands. That's why we should constantly be praying and asking him for help. He might not spare us from the consequences of a poor decision or something out of our control, but neither will he ever abandon us.

I say this because I've made some really bad decisions, and so have my friends and family. I've watched some messy situations unfold in front of my eyes. But never have I seen my family or friends abandoned by God. He's always right beside us, guiding us out of the muck we wandered into like witless goats. Sometimes it takes years to recover from dumb choices, so of course it's best to make good decisions early. But being a witless goat is hardly a sin. Jesus isn't known as the Good Shepherd for nothing, you know.

Our kids are in middle school, which means we have a few short years to get ready for college. Audrey seems to think this is ridiculous because college is a distant dream, but Eric and I know how quickly these years will pass. Soon she'll have a job and a driver's license, and then she'll be taking entrance exams and visiting colleges and we'll be filling out the federal financial aid paperwork that our friends cry about every spring. I hear it's horrible. I hear that it takes hours and hours to prove to the government that you're broke and your child needs tons of grants.

All of this delight awaits us. We're keenly aware of the costs of college and the ways it could all go so terribly wrong. The last thing we want is for our kids to live in our basement and wait for us to take care of them forever, but the second-to-last worst thing is that they graduate from college with $150,000 in debt and then go to work at the fast food joint down the hill. That would be awful. And the third worst thing that could happen is that the economy crashes, we all lose our jobs, and the four of us end up living in one of the outbuildings on a family farm. There's no end to the terrible options of the future.

We need to help our kids carefully navigate all the possibilities, but we also need to trust. We need to walk in faith. All of this will pass away, so we need a steady focus on what God has promised.

"So be strong and courageous!" Moses said to God's people as he turned over leadership of Israel to Joshua. "Do not be afraid and do not panic before them. For the LORD your God will personally go ahead of you. He will neither fail you nor abandon you. . . . Do not be afraid or discouraged, for the LORD will personally go ahead of you. He will be with you; he will neither fail you nor abandon you" (Deut. 31:6, 8). Don't you love how Moses repeated himself a little there? I mean, the guy was already 120 years old, so maybe that's part of it. But I think a bigger part was that he was trying to encourage a lot of scared people who were unsure about the future.

Just like us. Our agonizing about the future isn't going to help anything, so maybe we need to rest in our God who will never fail or abandon us. There's no way we can ensure the future will turn out the way we want, but we have his promise that he'll be there with us.

And that must be enough for us.

Make It Personal

1. What is one decision you've made that you would have made differently with knowledge of the future? What is one event, completely out of your control, that changed the plans you had made? What happened with that decision and event?

2. What current decision or possible catastrophe are you agonizing over? What's the worst thing that could happen? What are some specific ways God could hold you steady even if the outcome is something you fear?

Scripture Focus

"Seek the Kingdom of God above all else, and live righteously, and he will give you everything you need. So don't worry about tomorrow, for tomorrow will bring its own worries. Today's trouble is enough for today" (Matt. 6:33–34).

A Prayer for Today

Dear Father, I accept that you alone set the time for all future events. I accept that you alone have the knowledge of all that has happened and all that will happen. I only ask that you give me the ability to make wise decisions with my limited human understanding. I want to honor you in all things; may your loving hand guide me always. Amen.

It's Possible the World Does Not Revolve Around Me

On Pride

I THINK IT's the way she tosses her hair. She has this long, beautiful hair she somehow curls *just so*, which makes giant, soft waves roll over her shoulders—like something out of a movie. It's certainly her hair.

But it's also the way she sashays through the school, cell phone in hand. Her followers saunter behind her, although their hair isn't quite so spectacular and their mincing steps aren't quite so practiced.

Whatever it is, every time I go to my kids' school and see this woman-child, I mutter to myself, "Someone needs to take that kid down a peg."

Forgive me, Lord, for I have been unkind. But I have not been wrong. Not in this case, at least.

Middle schoolers are not really known for their humility or ability to tone themselves down, so this girl isn't the only one who needs a reality check. They're wild, spazzy, attention-seeking children in adult-sized bodies. I know—I live with two of them and they bring their friends over in a never-ending rotation. Middle school is happening in its full glory, right here in my very own house. Pray for me.

Not that I'm complaining. I'll take a passel of middle schoolers over a baby any day. Any day, do you hear me? Middle school kids sleep all night and take their own showers. They fold their own clothes and have full, intelligent conversations.

Well, they have the capacity for full and intelligent conversations. Whether they put their faculties to use or not depends on the day. But even on their worst days, I find my middle school–aged children and their friends to be a delight. Ish. Delight-ish is probably most accurate. There are other days I want to throw myself from the minivan on the drive to school, I admit.

Back in the day I faced my own set of popular girls with mincing steps and too-cute giggles. One of the worst offenders, a girl who wedged her ninety-pound body into designer jeans every day of middle school and high school, took early 1990s hair to an art form. Her hair was high; her hair was wide. Her hair was permed and teased and fried. I rolled my eyes daily behind her tiny, delicate back.

After we graduated and left that part of life behind, our mothers became friends. I didn't even know the girl had a mother; I'd assumed she'd been spawned in some dark underworld. No, wait. I do remember one day in high school when I heard her complaining about her mother to a friend. She used the B-word, which I didn't even know a person could use about her mother without being struck dead immediately. Nothing happened. No lightning or plagues or anything.

So, yes, she did have a mother, who turned out to be a very nice woman. And so for twenty years I've gotten periodic updates on Tiffany's life (of course that's not her real name). My mom says things like, "Did you hear Tiffany moved to the big city and fell in love?" "Did you hear she married into a wealthy family?" "Did you hear she's had her third baby and still weighs less than a sparrow?"

No, Mom. I hadn't heard. But thanks oh so much for the update. Wonderful. Forgive me while I roll my eyes at her from five hundred miles away.

Not that my own life has turned out badly—I love my life. I weigh considerably more than a sparrow and my husband's family isn't wealthy, unless you count acres owned as cash in the bank. But we're doing quite nicely, thank you. Yet, if I'm going to be completely honest, I'm still waiting for the news that something in this girl's life hasn't turned out perfectly. I'm still waiting for her to be taken down a peg, as cruel and un-Christlike as that is.

Middle school scars fade slowly, I guess. I don't excuse my terrible attitude, but I do recognize it for what it is—the universal need to know that, in the end, everyone has their own set of troubles and challenges. It's not that I want to feel better than everyone else, but I certainly don't want to feel less than anyone either.

This subconscious pride causes all manner of stress. It causes me to speak in ways that are cruel and selfish (as you have just plainly seen). It quietly whispers, "Me first, me first," in my mind and encourages me to make decisions based on my own desires and feelings. I forget to care for others and to listen before I speak. I become silently competitive, ranking my skills and good fortune against others.

It's gross. I gross myself out with my own selfishness. Sometimes a wave of physical nausea washes over me when I realize how self-centered I am. It feels awful, but at the same time I'm terribly grateful for it. I've been following Christ for enough years to recognize this gross feeling for what it actually is—conviction. The Holy Spirit is breaking through my sin, calling me to repentance and grace.

> I've been following Christ for enough years to recognize this gross feeling for what it actually is—conviction.

I don't have to wallow in my own selfishness. I can repent and be restored.

I don't mean to sound melodramatic here. But isn't it true that our deepest hurts have been caused when someone else listened to the little "me first, me first" voice in their heads? Talk to the wife who's been abandoned and left to raise the children alone. Her husband decided Me First was a pretty good idea and walked out the door. Think of the employer who's had thousands of dollars stolen from his bank account. His employee decided Me First needed a bigger paycheck. Consider the children who grow up in drug-addicted homes. Me First decided evenings were best spent in a chemical haze, no matter what the children needed.

Me First destroys lives. If we let it, it'll destroy our lives and the lives of those we love. That's why we need to do anything to make sure we're ignoring Me First with everything we have within us. After repenting of where we've already failed, we choose to seek what's best for others. We listen instead of forcing our own opinions. We choose gentle words instead of irritated shouts. We pray instead of manipulating. "You first" becomes the anthem of our heart.

To the world this makes no sense. It doesn't understand servanthood instead of power-grabbing. It doesn't understand mercy instead of retribution. The world doesn't naturally welcome, share, or love. It finds Jesus's ways foreign, because Jesus never let pride or selfishness make his decisions.

Philippians 2:5–8 tells us to "have the same attitude that Christ Jesus had. Though he was God, he did not think of equality with God as something to cling to. Instead, he gave up his divine privileges; he took the humble position of a slave and was born as a human being. When he appeared in human form, he humbled himself in obedience to God and died a criminal's death on a cross."

Humility, slavery, and a criminal's death don't sound that great to us. *They sound awful.* Why would we be interested in living like this? Because in that mysterious way God has, humility and even death are turned into something beautiful and far bigger than ourselves. He sees our hearts and is able to make eternal and glorious things happen for his glory.

The second part of that passage from Philippians goes on to say, "Therefore, God elevated him to the place of highest honor and gave him the name above all other names, that at the name of Jesus every knee should bow, in heaven and on earth and under the earth, and every tongue declare that Jesus Christ is Lord, to the glory of God the Father" (vv. 9–11).

Jesus didn't elevate himself. He didn't choose the way of pride or self-centeredness. He humbled himself, and then his Father lifted him up.

I don't understand the peace that comes from choosing God's way over my own selfishness. I just know I've experienced it and it's the best feeling this side of heaven. Surrender is hard. But repentance and humility turn into something more beautiful than one pitiful woman trying (and often failing) to follow Jesus's example. God's glory shines through us and right into the lives of the people around us. He elevates us for his own glory.

There's something freeing about turning from ourselves. The stress recedes when we stop idolizing ourselves. Constantly demanding our own way is futile, and idolizing ourselves is exhausting because it makes us responsible for things we can't possibly handle. There's a better way to live, even though it involves following a Savior who thought humility and death were legitimate options.

I don't claim to understand how it works; I only know it does. There is peace, freedom, and relief in self-sacrifice. I'll take those over being able to wedge a sparrow-sized body into Guess jeans any day.

Make It Personal

1. Do you still remember the girl in middle school who pranced around with perfect hair? Are you still irritated at her? How has her treatment of other people affected how you view and treat others?
2. Identify a way your pride could be causing pain to another person, and then pray over how you can repair that relationship.
3. Think of two people who put the needs of others above their own desires. What kind of blessings did their choices bring to others? How can you incorporate their examples into your own life?

Scripture Focus

"Is there any encouragement from belonging to Christ? Any comfort from his love? Any fellowship together in the Spirit? Are your hearts tender and compassionate? Then make me truly happy by agreeing wholeheartedly with each other, loving one another, and working together with one mind and purpose. Don't be selfish; don't try to impress others.

Be humble, thinking of others as better than yourselves. Don't look out only for your own interests, but take an interest in others, too" (Phil. 2:1–4).

A Prayer for Today

Heavenly Father, how can I be so relentlessly selfish? I see the damage that it causes. I know the times I've been hurt from others' self-centered choices. Please forgive me and help me to truly take an interest in what is best for others. I long for the peace that comes from surrendering my own way. Amen.

The End, Amen.

Conclusion

A FEW YEARS ago, our friends decided to adopt. The first son came home straight from the hospital, and a few years later so did his half brother. It took a few years for everyone to realize the extent of the boys' special needs, which include autism, delayed development, and ADHD. They're wonderful, fun, sweet boys, but caring for them daily takes everything our friends have and, honestly, a whole lot more. Isaac and Kelly are running on tanks that emptied out about four years ago, with no end in sight.

They're dealing with every kind of stress, fermenting into a bubbling, breathing, daily stew. They're handling normal adulthood with things like bills and laundry, but then the boys' needs add stress that won't let up. And on top of it all, they battle their own needs and human nature. It's tough.

I come home from visiting them emotionally undone. Like, for days. I just wander around my house, randomly yelling things like, "How can they bear that stress? It's so unfair." I'm crushed by how easy my kids are in comparison, and I don't know how I'd be able to hold up if I'd been given kids with extensive special needs.

Kelly sent me a link to a blog post about moms of autistic kids who suffer from stress so severe it's similar to the post-traumatic stress endured by soldiers after they leave combat.[9] These moms find they can never relax, even when they're alone in Target or trying to take a nap. Their daily strain affects them in permanent ways. The blog post referenced a news story of a mother in Oregon who threw her autistic son over a bridge when she simply could not take the pressure any more. Her own mental health had been rocky, and there wasn't enough support in their community to keep their little family safe or functioning. In the end she made a drastic, permanent decision, driven there by needs she could not meet.[10]

I don't have an autistic child, but I can completely see how a mother could get to that spot. I have nothing but compassion and grace for the loads some of us bear. I'd crumple too.

After I get home from our friends' house, I also spend a few days trying to figure out how to help them, or how to fix the situation for them. I could show up and clean the house or do the laundry or babysit or something, but honestly, when am I supposed to fit that into my life? I have two spots of time left—I can quit my job or quit sleeping. Neither option is workable.

I'm not even sure that helping would help. When our family shows up with our two (mostly) normal children and our easy marriage and our regular income, it probably feels like a punch straight to Isaac and Kelly's kidneys. Our "help" might feel more like bleach powder rubbed straight into their exhausted, endless wounds. And what about our other friends who carry heavy loads? How do I help one family and not the other? I can't pay all the bills, babysit all the children, or manage their chaos for them.

Let's take a moment to consider how completely insufferable I am, assuming I can help, fix, or manage them. Who do I think I am? God? I can't find any place in the Bible that tells me that I'm supposed to take those burdens on myself. I serve Christ; I am not Christ. Henri Nouwen has this to say on the subject in his book ¡Gracias!, as he considered the grief that several family members experienced after they lost loved ones.

I now feel tired and emotionally drained. As I let all these pains in the lives of my family and friends enter into my heart,

I wondered how I could offer true comfort. How could I ever enter into their pain and offer hope from that place? How could I enter into real solidarity with them? But then I slowly realized that I do not have to be like them or to carry their burdens, but that our Lord, my Lord and their Lord, has carried all human burdens and was crushed by them, so that we could receive his Spirit, the comforter. I realize now that my first task is to pray that this comforting Spirit will reach the hearts and minds of all those to whom I have written today. I hope that my halting and stuttering letters will be received as an expression of my sincere prayer that what is beyond my ability to touch can be touched by the consoling and healing power of the God whose name is Love.[11]

This is exactly what I'm coming to realize. I can't fix things for my loved ones. I can't heal them or go to the deepest places that only the Holy Spirit can tend. But I can pray for them. I can lift them up to the one who can make broken things whole, the one who provides everything out of nothing. I can intercede to the heavens when my friends need more than I was ever designed to deliver.

And I can show up. You can show up. We can't deliver what only God can do, but we can show up with whatever equipment God has given us. You may show up with casseroles or cakes. Cleaning supplies or a wrench. I show up with my words, because almost no one wants my casseroles.

I'd like to take a moment to publicly acknowledge that I have been avoiding, for some years now, our church's meal-planning team. If you have had a baby or a surgery in our congregation in the last ten years, I have failed you by ignoring emails and Facebook posts and websites designed with extensive sign-up lists. But trust me, if I had brought you a meal, I also would have failed you. It's better for everyone this way.

So I can't bring a decent casserole to save my life, but I can show up with my words. I can show up with my heart breaking over what breaks theirs. I can encourage, love, listen, and encourage some more. I want my friends to know they're awesome and they're doing a fabulous job and no one could do it better than they do. I hope this is enough. It's all I have. Well, sometimes I wash their dishes, because I'm pretty good at that too.

Showing up for our friends will mean that we share their load. This is different than fixing them and solving all their problems, but it does mean that what hurts them hurts us too. This is how the church should function—everyone working together to lighten each individual's burden. When we share our time, resources, and energy on behalf of our sisters and brothers in Christ, I believe we show our Father's love to a world that's watching and waiting to see if we have anything of value for them. A loving, giving church will radiate our Father's heart. Who wouldn't be attracted to that?

> This is how the church should function—everyone working together to lighten each individual's burden.

It may seem counterintuitive to show up for other's problems when we have enough of our own, thank you very much. If we're drowning, how on earth are we supposed to help another person who's also drowning? It feels like we're about to have a party on the sandy bottom of a very large, very terrible sea. We're all going down together.

But no. When the church acts like Christ called her to act, we don't falter. Our care and unity buoy us. Together we float, not sink. Jesus, just before he went to the cross, spent a lot of time reminding his followers of the most important things: "This is my commandment: Love each other in the same way I have loved you. There is no greater love than to lay down one's life for one's friends. . . . I appointed you to go and produce lasting fruit, so that the Father will give you whatever you ask for, using my name. This is my command: Love each other" (John 15:12–13, 16–17).

We've been appointed to bear lasting fruit and have been given the assurance of whatever we need for the task. Our command is simply to love one another. Show up. Bring the casserole or the cake if that's your thing. Bring your listening ears and your encouraging words and your prayers. Let's eat together in hospital waiting rooms and at funeral luncheons. Let's have picnics and housewarming parties and celebrations after the marriage ceremonies. Let's be in and out of each other's houses and lives, like little kids who all live on the same street.

It's this togetherness that brings wholeness. God works in and through our obedience and loves to fix what we can never manage on our own. I completely understand that if you're getting sucked into your own quagmire of stress, you may have no strength to reach out and help someone else. You might be far beyond your own strength. I get this. But I also believe that the Bible is true, and it tells us that a faithful, Christ-seeking life finds a tender spot in our Father's heart. He can work through us because "the eyes of the LORD search the whole earth in order to strengthen those whose hearts are fully committed to him" (2 Chron. 16:9). Showing up for your friends will help them, but it may also do beautiful things in your own life. You may get a front-row seat to God's work just by stepping past your own stress for the sake of a friend.

Our circumstances may not change, but our experiences of those circumstances can change radically. We can walk through life defeated, exhausted, and pecked down to a nub. Or we can choose another way. We can choose hearts that are fully committed to God. We can choose Christ's way of love and togetherness, forgiveness and humility. We can choose to lift these burdens and bills and people to God, and ask for his help this day.

It's my prayer that this will be true for you. Even if you wake up tomorrow in the same room, with the same autistic children, with the same stack of credit card bills on the counter, or in the same prison cell with the same terrible cellmates, your life can be completely different. Our lives don't have to look like this; we get to choose.

May we choose well, and may God fill in all the places we lack.

Epilogue

A LOT HAPPENS between the writing of a book and when you, my dear reader, actually get to read the book. I thought you might appreciate a few updates.

For those of you worried about Captain Kitty's well-being:

He's fine, I promise. He's alive and well and he now weighs at least sixteen pounds. But we did have to move him out to the garage this fall when he took to revenge pooping on the carpet. That was my last straw, and once again I had plans to have him euthanized instead of dropping him off, alone and terrified, at the shelter. But once again Eric talked me out of it. His exact words were, "I just don't think it's a good idea to teach the kids that if something poops in the house, we kill it." Oh, the man is just so sweet. So, we bought an extreme-weather heating pad for the Captain to sleep on, we make sure his cat door lets him outside when he wants to go, and when it snows really hard we put a little TV in the garage and let him watch *The Hobbit* on repeat. Sometimes I take a DVD of *The Golden Girls* out there, he jumps up on my lap, and we snuggle while watching it. I am not making that up.

For those of you wondering about my sister's wedding:

The wedding was perfect. It really was. All the pictures show us laughing and enjoying the event, even though we were well beyond our social limits and wearing uncomfortable shoes. The weather cooled down to a bearable level, no tornadoes destroyed anything earlier in the week (a real concern), and the guests all seemed to enjoy themselves very much. (And I found a great dress for fifteen dollars at my favorite resale shop. Woo-hoo!)

Thanks so much for reading, my friend. You mean so much to me. If you'd like to keep up with what's happening in the Clemence world, join me here:

Jessieclemence.com, where I blog about once a week
Facebook.com/jessieclemence
Instagram.com/jessieclemence
Twitter.com/jessieclemence4

I'd love to hear from you!

Jess

Notes

1. Mark W. Hamilton, ed., *The Transforming Word: One-Volume Commentary on the Bible* (Abilene, TX: Abilene Christian University Press, 2009), 553.
2. Madeleine L'Engle, *Walking on Water: Reflections on Faith and Art* (New York: Convergent Books, 2016), 61.
3. Ann Leary, "Home Alone," *Real Simple*, August 2016, 43–46.
4. Benjamin W. Labaree, *Colonial Massachusetts: A History* (Millwood, New York: KTO Press, 1979), 32–33.
5. Sophie Hudson, *Home Is Where My People Are: The Roads That Lead Us to Where We Belong* (Carol Stream, IL: Tyndale House Publishers, 2015), xiii.
6. Elizabeth Gilbert, *Big Magic: Creative Living Beyond Fear* (New York: Riverhead Books, 2015), 124.
7. Joshua Becker, *The More of Less: Finding the Life You Want Under Everything You Own* (Colorado Springs: WaterBrook, 2016), 170–71.
8. Jen Hatmaker, *For the Love: Fighting for Grace in a World of Impossible Standards* (Nashville: Nelson Books, 2015), 118.
9. Shawna Wingert, "Traumatic Stress and Autism Moms," *Not the Former Things* (blog), November 5, 2014, http://nottheformerthings.com/2014/11/05/traumatic-stress-and-autism-mommas/.
10. "Jillian McCabe Accused of Throwing Autistic Son Off Oregon Bridge," NBC News, November 4, 2014, http://www.nbcnews.com/news/us-news/jillian-mccabe-accused-throwing-autistic-son-oregon-bridge-n240606.
11. Henri Nouwen, *¡Gracias! A Latin American Journal* (Ossining, NY: Orbis Books, 1993), 33.